Mike McArthur

JESUS ABOUT

LOVING

YOURSELF

RELIGIOUS VIEW ON HOT TOPICS

IN PSYCHOLOGY

Mark 12:30-31 Love the Lord your God with all your heart and with all your soul and with all your mind and with all your strength.' The second is this: 'Love your neighbor as yourself.' There is no commandment greater than these.

WHY I WROTE THIS BOOK

I am absolutely sure that this book will help everyone to get to know yourself better and on a deeper level, improve your relationships, accept yourself and others, love your life and be happy while enjoying *"peace of mind,"* get rid of fear and stress, find the meaning of your life, solve different problems, and, finally, find God within you.

While reading this book you can find the answers to many of your questions because this book is based on the Bible, a universal book of life created by God and proven by billions of people of different nations for thousands of years.

All the relationships including all the problems in the relationships were given to you by God to show you that you need to learn how to love yourself. That is the main purpose of life. The only thing that we learn in this life is to love.

WHY YOU SHOULD READ THIS BOOK

What is loving yourself? There is always a misconception about it, but loving yourself is a most important thing in your life and this book will prove it. I am sure many of us have read the Bible; but so, fewer people actually understood very famous quote *Mark 12:31 "Love your neighbor as yourself."* If you really spend some time thinking about this phrase, maybe sleep on it, what do you think this phrase is about?

You should love yourself first. Always. You need to learn how to love yourself first, and only afterwards you could love your neighbor. Therefore, if you don't love yourself, it's not possible to love others. There is simply no such way. And this is a main problem in every romantic relationship. There is a common misconception nowadays that relationships are supposed to bring love to our life. When it doesn't happen, we become miserable.

The truth is that, according to the Bible, romantic relationships are never the source of love. Remember: Love your neighbor as yourself. First, you love yourself and only then you could love your boyfriend or girlfriend. So, true source of love is within us! Nowadays people are looking for love in the relationships without having love in their soul and, of course, they fail to find it.

Relationships are not a source of love, but a reflection of our soul and mind. Therefore, if we don't have a love in ourself, we are *never* going to find love in our relationships. And that is the word of Christ.

ABOUT EGO

❖

A lot of people think that you need to love others, not yourself, that loving yourself is having a huge ego. But, actually, ego is a result of not loving yourself. The term egotism is derived from the Greek ("εγώ") and subsequently its Latinized as ego – it means "a person who has ego." But who doesn't have an ego? There is no such person in the world without ego. I think the term ego is not exactly correct, it is better to use the word yourself, but we will use it because it is a word that we know more.

Simply to say that you an egoist is the same as to say you have two hands and two legs. Yes, everyone is an egoist because everyone has an ego, it's that simple. Very often those people who say that you have a big ego or you are a self-lover are actually huge self-lovers themselves.

In my understanding, egoist is an individual who knows his rank in the world, and will not accept any other different opinion about himself. An egoist can self-analyze and find out where he swamped compared to other people. Egoists also understand the true source of behavior and feelings of others.

As you see, being an egoist is a good quality. Let's agree to use another word for those who are thinking only for themselves with no regard of feelings or desires of others – egocentrics.

Egocentrics cannot wish to have concern or sympathy for others. They only have their own point of view, and have a bad understanding of other people and what motivates them. They don't observe inconvenience because they don't think about the needs of others.

But, in reality, an egocentric is a person who does not love himself. This might seem strange because a lot of us think that egocentrics love themselves too much. I affirm that an egocentric is a person who does not love himself but forces others to love him because he cannot love himself. But he is constantly seeking love to feel energized and rejuvenated. Love is a state of mind that gives you a lot of energy.

Because an egocentric is a person who does not love himself but he is eager to feel loved, the only way for him is to force others to give him that energy of love. Others need to do something for him to the prejudice of themselves.

Therefore, an egocentric is a person who desperately needs love, attention, and care because he cannot give such energies to himself and at the same time, he cannot live without it.

Egocentrism is having low empathy for feelings and needs of others, and feels no guilt about it. An egocentric sincerely does not understand that, in addition to his point of view, there may be another. Or even several different opinions. He lives by the principle: "There are two opinions, mine and wrong." An egocentric can be in relationships for years, and not even guess to put himself in the shoes of his partner.

I am pretty sure that each of us met such egocentrics in our life. The funny thing is that when such a person didn't get so much desired love or attention, he blames others of being egoists (selfish, having a huge ego, self-lovers, etc.). After finishing reading this book, you may always reply that yes, it is who I am, I have an ego, and I also have my own needs and it is okay.

What do you think are the people from all around the world afraid of the most? There was a poll asking this question to people from different countries and different ages, and by far the winner was loneliness. I am pretty sure you know that feeling of alienation, or exclusion. Even surrounded by your friends and relatives you can feel lonely. In the 21st century a lot of people are afraid of staying alone with their own thoughts. That's why there are so many articles on the Internet on where to spend your weekend, what parties, sports events to visit, what are the best movies or books of year, etc., just not to stay alone with your own thoughts.

What are you supposed to do with your thoughts? If you truly love yourself, it is okay stay alone, and to think in silence regularly about your life, life of others, or about the book that you have just read. So, let go of self-judgement because it is always ineffective and inaccurate. Acceptance of yourself without self-judgement is a great first step toward the loving yourself process.

So, stop seeing loneliness as something negative. There's nothing wrong with lonely people. It is not a flaw or something shameful. Actually, there was a psychologic study published in Cognition and Emotion that found that loneliness actually has an adaptive function that serves humanity. So, from an evolutionary point of view, it motivates us to find really deep and loving connections.

❖

ACTION POINTS:

• Remember the last time you enjoyed time alone: walk in the park, exercise without listening to music, finding a time for thinking about life, or just simply staring at the window without an active thinking process

• Try to find a time for enjoying time alone. Allow you to be alone with yourself and stay present for at least half an hour a day, you can do any activity from the above

LACK OF LOVE

❖

John 4:11 Beloved, if God so loved us, we ought also to love one another.

❖

We as a human race that lives in the 21st century are afraid that we will run out of food, gas, power, etc., but in reality lack of most resources in our life is love. And, first, the total shortage of love of ourself. And we have a situation where many musicians sing about love, writers write about love, we are watching romantic movies about it, but not many of them experienced such feeling because they don't have it in ourself, in our soul and mind.

Therefore, it doesn't make any sense to worry about the relationship, drink wine, and complain to your friends; instead put all your energy in loving yourself and relationships will come as a reflection of your soul and mind.

Relationships is a #1 problem in our world (by far), because of this misconception. It's a common mistake, confusion of cause with effect. And the solution of this problem is to read the Bible carefully. This book gives you a clear understanding of what is cause and what is effect and ability to see the truth. And that's a main goal of your life.

Not loving yourself causes lack of love in your love, problems with relationships; this, in turn, causes feeling miserable. Such unhappiness influences the whole life, and as a result, a person not to love himself even more and more. This is a source of a psychological problems. Such problems may end up with alcoholism, being on drugs, or feeling depressed, which is also a huge psychological problem.

Depression is a self-hate for not being good enough for the perfection that you have in your mind. When you are depressed, you might think you not beautiful enough, not tall enough, you have huge nose, etc. And this is also a big deal in the modern world. I personally know girls in their early 20s who have been on antidepressants for years! And it is only a beginning of their life; what will happen next? According to a study by the National Center for Health Statistics (NCHS), the rate of antidepressants' use in the USA among teens and adults (people ages 12 and older) increased by almost 400% between 1988–1994 and 2005–2008. Overall, one in six Americans take some kind of psychiatric drugs — mostly antidepressants, they wrote in the *Journal of the American Medical Association.*

And this data does not count other addictions, such as alcohol, drugs (cocaine, opioids, etc.), and everything that is supposed to make you "relaxed." Drug overdose deaths have more than tripled since 1990. About 5 million Americans are regular cocaine users. More than 90% of people who have an addiction started to drink alcohol or use drugs before they were 18 years old. About 6% of American adults (about 15 million people) have an alcohol use disorder, but only about 7% of Americans who are addicted to alcohol ever receive treatment

And the source of these errors is a lack of knowledge of self-love by the vast majority of people. I've seen many people in the grocery store who buy the best food and clothes for their pets. They might spend several minutes reading the ingredients section for the cat food. They want all the best for their pets while buying cheapest food for themselves. On the contrary, a person who truly loves himself is very strict on his own diet. You can say that ascetics are the ones who love themselves most. I am not saying you should become ascetic and live on bread and water, but think about how eating too much or eating junk food leads to you not loving your body when looking at it in front of the mirror or body shaming yourself. But a lot of people allow themselves to eat too much sugar products, drink alcohol, consume junk food, not having physical exercise, etc., everything that leads to an unhealthy lifestyle.

The problem is that our society thinks that is a sign of self-love; but it's an opposite, self-hate. This is something that destroys your body, your health, and, as a result, makes your life shorter. Is this a what true self-lover does to himself?

Sometimes people seriously can eat expired food just not to throw it in a trash can. So, they treat their body as a place that is worse than trash. Is it an act of self-love? Another situation is when we eat much more than we should, just not to throw the food out.

If such an individual treats himself very badly, how do you think he will treat you? Because your relationship will be a reflection of his self-love within his soul and mind. So, people start their relationships hoping to get love from a partner, but they cannot get it, which causes a long list of claims to your partner. No love in your soul and heart will result in no love in life. No self-love will result to no love of others. That's God's law from the Bible.

❖

ACTION POINTS:

• Think and answer the question honestly: Do I really love myself? If yes, up to what percentage? ... 20 or 30 percent out of 100? When finish reading this book, I encourage you to answer the same question again.

• Think about how excluding all the junk and unhealthy food would make your life better? Write top 5 benefits for your health, energy, and overall perception of life.

• Write top 5 benefits to your life by excluding alcohol, cigarettes, or any other drugs that destroy your body and mind.

• Think about situations in your life when you've felt depressed. How would exactly developing your inner connection to God help you in that kind of situation?

WHAT IS LOVE

❖

John 4:7 Anyone who does not love does not know God, because God is love

❖

Love is an energy, and if you don't have a source of love in your soul and mind, this will cause several enormous problems in your life.

Everything started from God and God created a human, granted him life, and God is love. If you don't have a love in your soul and mind, which is reflected in lack of loving yourself, it unfortunately means you don't have God within you.

That's why in any religion there is a rite similar to baptism, where a child is initiated into a religion, and from that moment it's attached to God. And in some cultures, godparents are viewed to be more important to the child then real ones! But nowadays unfortunately there is not so many people with God in their soul and mind. And that's a source of all problems in our life.

Earlier, even 100 years ago, when someone has a problem he would probably go to the church, to tell the God about it. But now, we are going to the psychologists, who have exactly the same problems in their life. The only way to solve your problems is to find love within you, which means to find your connection to God.

Not loving yourself means you don't have a God in your soul and mind. Not having God within you means that you don't have energy to achieve your dreams because love is an energy. You only have unfulfilled desires. Loving yourself is a reflection of loving God because God created man in his own image. If you don't love yourself you don't love God within you.

This simply means that you don't really trust in God. The trust starts with how you treat yourself. God created you with love, and how do you treat his divine creation? If you treat yourself badly, sorry, but you don't truly believe in God. And moreover, if you don't love yourself, you cannot love anyone and anything else, you simply don't have such material.

One of my favorite verses is "God is love" from John the Baptist. This quote is really stuck in my head and affects all of my life since I've read it. And, truly loving yourself means loving God within you.

The common mistake is that when people are looking for relationships, they truly are looking for love of themselves. And what other person can love you more than yourself? No one. Sooner or later people will find it out. The more you will be forced to love in the relationships, and this is what egocentrics do, unfortunately the more miserable you will be, the more "hate" you will have toward your boyfriend or girlfriend because they cannot love you more than yourself, and the more "hate" you will have to yourself because you don't have the love within you.

If you would have a love within you and your soul and mind, you could share it with your partner by focusing on giving, not taking. You cannot take love from your partner because most probably he or she would have the same problem with absence of self-love. That's why only unconditional love is an answer to all of the relationship problems.

❖

ACTION POINTS:

• Take the time to think about verse is "God is love" from John the Baptist. What does it mean to you? What emotions does it cause within you? Write you answer

• Think about how having God within your mind and soul will help you to love yourself more.

UNCONDITIONAL LOVE

❖

John 4:19

We love because he first loved us.

❖

This is a perfect kind of love about which all of us have dreamed and what we seek and unfortunately not many of us happen to find.

We can understand it literally as love without conditions and restrictions, when you are loved just because you exist and just because of who you are. One important thing is that to love unconditionally first you need to love and accept yourself.

This is a love that our parents love us, especially a mother's love of her child. it does not depend on how beautiful your child is, how smart he is, how successful he is, etc., a mother will always love her child.

Ancient Greeks called it "Agape." It's a highest form of love, unconditional love, that is capable of sacrifice. They thought it's like a charity. and "the love of God for man and of man for God."

In our relationships, not each of us have experienced this feeling but sometimes we are lucky to find it. People who felt unconditional love from their parents subconsciously can give it to their partners. They have been raised in the family where parents loved them despite their grades in school, behavior, or success in life. Those people grow up with a clear understanding that they will be loved no matter what and they don't have to do anything to earn the love.

But despite that great background, sometimes we can meet the difficulties; for example, illusions. Let's say we mismatch our own ambitions to see some sort of perfection in our partner with feelings to love him just because of who he is.

You need to understand that your partner has a different character and he/she should not be the same as you. This is an acceptance of your partner. Pure love is freedom to love and accept your partner without conditions and restrictions.

This is a freedom for both lovers to be who they are when no one controls and forces you.

Unconditional love is the only real love that gives space to both partners to grow and develop themselves together. The need to be right and control the relationship creates a destructive relationship.

Those healthy relationships are more than just feelings and emotions, rather a conscious choice to help each other no matter what. It's a choice to give love, open your heart, accept each other, and be grateful for everything that you have in your life.

When you give love, you get it back. Relationships are a partnership that requires healthy borders, so no one can use each other.

Judgement and criticism destroy love by making it conditional. When you judge you partner you do not fully accept him. So, refusing to judge, being grateful, is one of the best ways to express your love and kindness. Mother Teresa once said, "If you will judge someone you will have no time to love him."

Ability to openly communicate to each other, respect our boundaries, is a sign of unconditional love. If you are ready to talk and to understand each other, finding a decision that will satisfy both of you in a conflict situation is also a sign of unconditional love. Try to find similarities in your relationships.

❖

ACTION POINTS:

• What does it mean to you to love unconditionally? Can you name examples of unconditional love in movies, novels, romantic songs?

• What sort of illusions in the relationships that we talked about in this chapter (see perfection in the partner, understanding different character of your partner) have you faced?

NO ONE CAN LOVE ME MORE THAN MYSELF

❖

John 15:12: "My command is this: Love each other as I have loved you."

❖

Love is God. People looking for love it means that they actually looking for God in the relationships. But it's a common mistake that happiness and love exist only in the relationships. If you have a relationship with someone, then you are kind of happy. And if you don't have a relationship, then you unhappy. Love and happiness are God and God is not in the relationships for such people.

And, of course, they couldn't find God in the relationships. If you have ever talk to someone who is thinking about divorce, you have seen a long list of claims for their partners. That's a result of looking for love in the relationships. Once again there is no God in the relationships, he is only inside you. In the relationships you have affection, attachment, addiction, maybe even gratitude, but not the main thing, the thing for which those people were actually looking.

You can only find true love if you have God in your soul and mind. And love cannot disappear simply because it's God. He is eternal. Isaiah 9:6 calls God an "Everlasting Father." Psalm 145:13 refers to God's kingdom as everlasting: "Your kingdom is an everlasting kingdom, and your dominion endures throughout all generations."

That's why the love is eternal in the relationships for true self-lovers. Love cannot dissolve. Disappeared love means that it was not love but something from the list of affections, attachments, addictions, marriage of convenience, sincerity, common interests, etc. You can finish this long list based on your own experience.

If we are being hurt from insecure relationships, we need to find a remedy for these psychological traumas in order to experience the true love of God the Father.

Those who are securely connected to God are not as frustrated by devastation, periods of questioning yourself, or misery. Even though one can feel remoteness from God or a partner, a recollection of when they came through in the past can bring back a sense of attachment.

And if you don't have God in your soul and mind you will not have relationships, money, and happiness because it means that you not connected to God and his energy. Simply put, you are not on his list. And the Creator can live without us, but it's extremely hard for us to live without him. In that case, we're fully on our own, no help from outside.

That's why there is always a rite of passage, an initiation into every religion, similar to the baptism, because without the acceptance from God we are not considered as good enough to be called humans by every religion. By the level of consciousness, we are then equal to animals that only think about what to eat, where to sleep, and nothing else. So, the sacred meaning of these initiating rites is to find the connection to God, and enter the kingdom of the Lord to be good enough to call yourself a "human."

Baptism, for example, is considered to be a form of rebirth —"by water and the Spirit"— that is why you have to be naked as in original birth. All of the rites of passage configure an individual to God and obliged him to follow the path to the God of his religion.

❖

ACTION POINTS:

• Try to analyze your past relationships. Was it a true love or more related to affections, attachments, addictions, marriage of convenience, sincerity, common interests?

• Write your own thoughts on how having God in your soul and mind would help you to find a true love in your life or to have a better relationship than in the past

QUESTION ON LOVING YOURSELF #1

❖

Can you really say no? Answer honestly.

How do you feel when saying no?

The thing is that an individual who truly is a self-lover allows himself say no easily.

But there is a sort of person who can't say "no" to anyone. They always pull weight not only for themselves, but also for the others: service for the coworkers, help relatives, accident, and frankly, not-needed orders from their boss and boss of others.

If feeling the inner barrier when saying "no," this is a subconscious mind working, we "sort of" say no, but inside we feel not good. Why is it so?

First and foremost, try to understand your motivation. What do you get for yourself personally when you do all the orders of your boss or help coworkers to your own detriment? Think on it. Just question yourself and listen to your own feelings and thoughts. Answering this question can help you to find alternative ways of reaction that may help you to feel your same needs another way.

But maybe you can change those needs. Maybe you already have everything inside you but you keep trying to help everyone to your own detriment?

The second step is also not easy. Try to take a break without responding. Before saving the work for your coworker or editing quarterly report of your coworker for the fifteenth time, stop and think – can you afford it? Maybe you can let others be a hero?

Start to learn how to say "no." First you can say it in easy situations, when you would reject to help others anyway. Just practice that your first reaction would be "no." Then, when saying your answer, you will still be saving the planet for your relatives and coworkers; but first, "no." You can say "sorry," you can try to pretend it is a joke, but the main thing is that all of your surroundings will get used to a new you who can reject them. Who knows, maybe this would be enough?

The most important thing is to start to manage all of your requests. You can take some requests, or delegate them to others. Be honest to yourself. If a favor from your coworker is to your own detriment, at least acknowledge it. Then you can start to say it out loud.

Here are some examples on how exactly you can say "no."

One of the most popular rejections is appeal to intent: "Do you want me to edit this report once again so we will not meet the deadline of signing this document?" All right, I will help you out, but you will talk to the manger to pay me for those extra hours, okay?"

Or "do you want me stay at work for two more hours? What will I get for it?" "What do you think if I will do your job instead of mine, will I get bonus?" etc. Talk about the essence of the favor, but nicely and with respect to the others.

Another way of saying "no" is to reschedule the favor under better conditions: "Okay, I will do it after I finish my own tasks" "Yes, course I will do it one more time, after signing the document," " I am ready to change this report if you can show me what needs to be changed," "I will help you out but instead you will give a call to all of my clients."

Another thing is "transfer of responsibility." It is a very soft way of rejection. If it is hard for you to decide, help others or not, let them decide. "I don't really know... We have two tickets to an opera, we've been waiting for this for a half a year..." "What should I do?" "I have a task for the next 3 hours and it's already an end of the working day. I have a deadline until tomorrow... My boss gonna kill me!" If your coworker does not want to realize you also have your own interests, you need to remind him softly.

The rude but sometime necessary way is to talk about the boundaries of responsibilities. This is the case when more soft ways don't work. You need to think about who you are for those who constantly are trying to ask you for a favor? How do they really treat you? "This is not my responsibility," "this is not my direct duty," "I am not getting money for it," "This is out of my interests," etc. Yes, it not a very nice way to end a conversation and it hurts, but we already talked about it.

Try to say those phrases in front of the mirror or your friend who understands you. Catch your feelings and how comfortable you are. "No" should sound decisively like stating a fact. Feel like a free person when saying "no."
No shame, no guilt – you allowed to say no, it's your right. And it should be reflected in your voice, gestures, posture, in your feeling of allowing yourself to be right.

Keep practicing. You need to get used to anything in your life, not to mention something new to you.

❖

ACTION POINTS:

• Practice each way of saying "no" we talked above:

• Understanding your motivation, taking a break, practice saying "no," reschedule a favor, transfer of responsibility, talk about boundaries

• Catch and write your feelings at the moment when practicing each way of saying "no."

STATE OF MIND

❖

Love is a state of mind which has nothing to do with the mind.

— Bob Phillips

❖

Love is a state of mind where your mind and soul open and energy flows into your body. It's a source of energy for humans. That's why, for poets, writers, and composers, love is essential. But for regular people like you and me, love is a source of energy. The thing is we don't have a lot of energy and moreover we waste it on discussing our future plans instead of doing the actual things. And, therefore, we cannot achieve our goals because we waste the vast majority of our energy on discussing our future plans. We don't have enough energy and that's why we seek love like junkies. Love is an addiction for us. That's why addiction products like coffee, alcohol, and cigarettes are very popular among us. When we finally find our love, we feel energized, we even walk and sit differently. But when these feelings are over, because everything has a beginning and end, we feel exhausted, regrets, maybe even hatred. All of this is happening because people lack energy. We need stimulus. Love is acting like coffee: our nervous system is excited at the first sip, we feel a burst of strength, but after a while this effect is over and we again feel the same lack of energy. So, you drink a new cup of coffee again and again. For your whole life.

The main question is why does this happen? This happens because we don't have much energy. So, we live from one cup of coffee to another, because we don't have our own source of energy inside us. Why don't we have our own source of energy? Because people in general do not love themselves. As I mentioned before, love is a state of mind when energy flows into you more than usual. And because an average individual doesn't have love in his mind and soul, energy flows only in cases of external events like finding a relationship.

And these external events create an addiction from it like the one from coffee. That is why we constantly are looking for a relationship, and if we don't have and we feel a lack of love in our life and we are miserable, we displace it with new addiction like antidepressants, alcohol, cigarettes, etc. So, all of our life we feel addiction from love or other drugs.

If you feel bad without a relationship in your life, sorry, but that's a sign of addiction. It's like if you didn't drink a coffee in the morning: all day you will think about drinking that cup of coffee to feel energized.

So, this is not a real love, it's an addiction, and that's why having a good and healthy relationship is such a rare thing. The reason is a not having love in yourself, and that's why we seeking love from others.

The sad thing is that your partner cannot give it you, because he/she is in the same situation. So, everything is interconnected. Loving yourself is absolutely necessary for having healthy relationships. If you have love in your soul and mind, you will have love in your life.

Love is beginning with love of ourself. You don't need to love anyone else. Start with yourself. At first. It's the same as money. To give money to someone, you first need to have it in your wallet. And if you don't have the money within yourself, you cannot give it to anyone else. It is that easy.

You can only ask for the money like a homeless person. And that's exactly what we do! We only borrow the money from each other, and no one has it. And then we feel miserable and think, why I don't have any money? Why am I single? The root of this problem is a lack of love yourself. We don't have an energy for anything because we don't have love in our mind and soul.

It is like you have a car, but don't have gas, and you have this car staying in your garage. Potentially, you can drive it to everywhere, but in the reality it's out of fuel. Love is your fuel, your source of energy.

Love is life. If you have love you have energy, so you have a life. If you don't have love, you don't have love in every aspect of your life; it's like having a car without fuel. It's useless.

QUESTION ON LOVING YOURSELF #2

❖

If you ask someone "Do you love yourself?", the answer will be most probably "Of course." But I have a personal criterion for determining whether an individual loves himself or not.

Do I accept who I am, or not always? Do I really want to change something inside me? Were there any previous events in your life that you feel guilty about, something that you don't want to remember?

Are there some flaws in your character that you don't really like? It's like asking which hand do you like most, left or right?

If you think it's a ridiculous question, then how can't you love some parts of your character, or parts of your body such as nose, eyes, breast? Isn't your nose, legs, or breast a part of you? And if you don't like those parts of you, it means you don't like the whole you; because it's all parts of your body.

And the same is with character: if you do not accept some parts of your character, you don't accept yourself as a whole. What exactly does it mean not to accept yourself? In reality, it means you don't love yourself. If you don't love the parts of you, you don't love yourself. It's that easy.

If you don't like yourself in some situations, if you are unhappy with yourself, if you don't like your behavior, then you don't like yourself. And if you don't love yourself, you don't have love in your soul and mind.

So, ask those questions to yourself honestly.

You may ask should I be okay with everything, like drinking too much alcohol or eating a lot of sugar? Earlier I wrote that having bad habits is a result of not loving yourself. So, you need to figure out what is a main motivation for having bad habits – self-hate or self-love? In this situation, there are only two answers: love or hate. And if you don't like yourself, the main motivation of your actions will be self-hate. Hating yourself is like declaring a war on yourself. You simply cannot quit bad habits like smoking, drinking, being drug addicted, etc., if your main motive is not loving yourself.

To prove this point, let's consider alcoholics. An alcoholic is a person who is miserable in his life. He is unhappy because of lack of love in his life. And lack of love in his life is a result of having lack of love of himself. He tried to get the love from woman, but didn't succeed. Then he tried another source of love, in his opinion, alcohol. Alcohol is, in reality, a concentrated sugar. And this sweet taste is a reminder of love from our childhood. Our mind accepts all the emotions in the form of tastes. Love has a sweet taste. If you don't get love from real life via kisses, hugs etc., your body still needs it. That's why it craves alcohol to replace a true love.

So, all of the flaws in your character are showing us what needs to be changed. And chasing them is a good thing, but the most important question is are you trying to change your character based on self-love or self-hate? And that's a big difference. And, you cannot really deeply change your self if it is self-hate. This is a road to nowhere, because everything you will do with that attitude will make a situation worse.

The worst-case scenario is that those changes will lead to depression because you will not get what you want from yourself, and that is a main cause of depression. An individual wants to change something but those changes are destructive by their nature because life is getting worse, not better.

In the end, those actions will always lead to a bad result. And if I fight with my character flaws, I destroy myself. It doesn't mean you don't have to change for the better. But it's always important to remember that fighting with yourself will not lead to any good result.

Nowadays everyone knows of their flaws in character, we fight with them for years and years, and we don't get any results. It's because if you fight with your flaws, you fight with yourself! I personally don't know many people who changed at least some flaws in their characters with that attitude.

I recommend that you always find the cause of our character flaws. And if we can find a source of these flaws, we will see that it always is the same. Yes, you named it — it's a lack of loving yourself. Because loving yourself means loving God within you. And that's why loving yourself is an answer to all of your problems.

ACTION POINTS:

• What is a self-acceptance to you? Can you call yourself a fully self-accepted person?

• Have you ever tried to find flaws in your character and tried to change yourself? What was the result of those changes?

• Write at least 10 sentences starting with the words: "I like myself for..."Also look for good things in people you dislike. In addition to developing positivity in perceiving what is happening, you will find it easier to find positive things in yourself. It is not necessary to write any huge merits here. Pay attention to any little things.

•

• This exercise is recommended to be performed daily for 1-2 months.

NOT ACCEPTING YOURSELF

❖

And God created man in his own image, in the image of God he created him; male and female he created them.

Genesis 1:27

❖

If I don't like myself, it means I don't like God. It's the same if I don't like the car means I don't like the factory where it was assembled. Because the factory is a cause and a car is an effect. The same is here, if I don't like myself, I don't like God the creator.

Here comes the question: Why don't I like some parts of my character or parts of my body? It's because it's not aligned with my personal wishes on how I should look or what my perfect life should be. Especially nowadays in the era of Instagram, social networks and influencers are a common problem.

Now there are profiles of "successful" people whose life shines like a diamond. You can have beautiful cars, expensive hotels, meals at fancy restaurants. You can see amazing dresses and jewels. But this is all fake life.

This fake life is very popular all around the world, not only in the U.S. The reason behind it may be different, but mostly it's bloggers who are earning money from their profile and interested in looking wealthy and the most attractive. Or, it can be entrepreneurs who need their clients to trust them. Teenagers, housewives whose virtual life with large amounts of subscribers, likes, and comments increase self-confidence and brings joy.

Keep in mind that anyone can create an illusion of a happy and wealthy life. Those people are among us. Do not think that your life is worse than someone's just because of their profile in the social networks. They create an image of a perfect life, but it's okay if your life is different.

What is more real is the image of you that you wish to be or the actual you? So, you love the more perfect you, your dreams, but not yourself. And you are just a defective attachment to the perfection.

And that's why plastic surgery is a very popular now. It's a direct result of not accepting parts of your body and not loving yourself.

What is plastic surgery? I am not talking about necessary operations when, for instance you have a broken nose or there is a real problem that interferes your regular life. I am talking about attempts to remake you, become a different person with the help of a knife. You might think that spending more money or suffering more will replace the feel of not loving yourself that's sitting inside. You think that if you do it you will *feel* differently. But we understand this is not true.

Another thing is trying to get rid of not loving yourself via love of your partner. A lot of people depend on how their partner treats them. In this case that individual thinks: if others will love me, I can finally love myself. If I feel adored and desired, I can suddenly feel beautiful. Sorry, but it is not going to work. That's why shyness and loneliness is a feeling inside. No one can love you more than yourself.

And, finally, to be, rather than to seem. A person just denies living in a body with which he was born. He disagrees with his own "I," and trying to find something better. Look at the teenagers who love to wear piercing and tattoo, t-shirts with skulls, etc., it's the same thing. It is as if some external attribute such as new nose or new breasts will protect you from the outside world to become stronger, smarter, or luckier. Like if I get lean, change noses, then my personal life is going to change, I will find a better job or get new friends. As you see, it doesn't work.

There is only one way to live in peace with yourself – to love your body simply because it's yours. No one in the world has the same combination of skin color, hair and eyes, lips and legs, fingers and nose. That's what you have. That is who you are. And when you start to divide your body like "this nose is good, but chaw needs to be changed," you divide yourself into the parts, making your body as something abstract, not really yours. That is why loving yourself always starts with fully accepting yourself with all of your flaws and defects.

❖

ACTION POINTS

• Try "Praise yourself"exercise: Every day praise yourself for something. For a great ideas, for a successful deal, for showing endurance, etc. You might reply - "I have nothing to praise myself for" - that seem to sound like being too shy. For me, this is more a sign of laziness. Keep practicing.

TWO WAYS OF APPROACH

❖

Hatred stirs up conflict, but love covers over all wrongs.

Proverbs 10:12

❖

As we discussed earlier, nowadays the highest shortage is lack of loving yourself. No one can love us more that yourself, and soon or later almost each individual become unhappy, dissatisfied, disappointed. And this shortage of loving yourself is the main source of problems in all relationships, which is influenced on your health and your personal finance.

A person is seeking love of yourself in anyone but himself. But to seek love first you need to be love. That's the only way to attract love into your life.

If you ask a random person what exactly is love of yourself and how can I love myself? Most probably no one can find an answer to this question. Some on them will say it's like a being an egocentric. Love of yourself always starts with acceptance of yourself. Earlier I wrote that accepting yourself means accepting you as a whole with every flaw and merit you have, accepting every piece of your body.

For the sake of interest, ask this question to some of your friends: Are they happy with yourself? Are they happy with every aspect of their life, because life is just a reflection of your state of mind and accepting yourself means accepting your life?

Accepting yourself means that you have a healthy basis for further development to move forward in your life. In this case, all your actions will be based on love. If I fully accept myself, I know that I have some flaws, I know all of them, but I want to be a better version of myself. This is a healthy motivation for changes.

Otherwise, all of my actions will be not an improvement of myself, but fighting with myself, where I will be doomed to fail from the very beginning. And this is the main difference in two ways of approach to yourself and approach to your life. One: I love myself, I want to be a better version of myself. Two: I don't like myself; I don't accept myself; I fight with myself.

Sorry, but it is foolish if you fight with yourself. It's the same if your right hand will declare a war on your left hand and will win by cutting it off. Doesn't make any sense.

Self-love and self-hate is like shoulder angel and shoulder devil. One leads to positive changes in your life and be a better version of yourself and other leads to all the negativity, such as fighting with yourself, stress, miserableness, and eventually, depression.

The thing is that the vast majority of people consider relationships as a process when your partner owes you something just because of who you are and you definitely expect something from him. And when your partner doesn't meet those expectation, you have a feeling of dissatisfaction, miserableness, and sometimes even hatred to your lover.

How dare your partner behave not as you expected, despite you being beautiful, well educated, and having a great job? The answer is that it's because all these wonderful qualities and merits that you have were not for you, but for your partners. It's like a packaging: it's for the outside, not the inside. And when your partner does not appreciate that packaging, you start questioning yourself. This is a good example of a situation that was given to you by God to show you that in reality you don't really love yourself. You just made a request and waited for the response from your partner. If he/she will accept you, then you will love yourself. This is a conditional love, not a healthy relationship.

And if you do love yourself, it doesn't matter how your partner will evaluate you because you are happy with who you are. You don't make a request; you simply exist in this world. Your self-love does not depend on opinions of others, even your boyfriend. And that is the main difference between loving yourself and everything else.

But if your self-love depends on opinions of others, then you don't really love yourself and you seek acceptance of some of your qualities, skills, and merits from others, so that in the future, potentially, you can start to love yourself. As I wrote earlier, loving yourself means full acceptance of yourself.

If you have it, then it doesn't matter what the rest will think about you because others will always have their opinion about you no matter what. Unfortunately, you cannot please everyone, it is not possible. But, for some reason, it causes unhappiness, dissatisfaction, and even depression.

Why are people want to please others? Again, it's the same answer, because of lack of self-love, and the seeking love from the outside. And the less self-love they have, they more they need love from the outside. It's that simple.

Their actions are based not on self-love, but self-hate and fear of not being accepted by others. And this is a disaster in the life of billions of people from all over the world. The vast majority of depressions comes from that. And this is a direct way to being depressed and being miserable because it is not possible to please everyone. The more will you try to please others, the more others will find flaws inside you.

❖

ACTION POINTS:

• Try to remember the last times you were trying to be a better version of yourself in the past. Was your main motivation based on loving yourself or fighting with yourself?

• Make a list of top 5 actions to improve yourself and write how exactly self-love will help you to achieve your target in a better way.

DO NOT TREAT OTHERS LIKE YOUR OWN THINGS

❖

Above all, love each other deeply, because love covers over a multitude of sins.

Peter 4:8

❖

Funny thing is that people require something from others based on their perception of life. And those people become surprised and dissatisfied when others do something wrong, not with accordance to those requirements.

But why do we think that others should behave as we require? Who do we think we are to request it from others? We treat our girlfriends or boyfriends as our own thing. The problem here is that since both of the partners do not love themselves in reality, they force each other to love them instead of loving themselves! And your partner, even if he will try very hard, will never love you more than you love yourself. That's why it leads to a miserable life.

The main problem here is that people do not communicate well in their relationships. We have requirements and exceptions but we don't discuss them with our partners. But we cannot blame our partner on violation of agreements that don't exist.

When you are in the relationship I think it is crucial to discuss what expectations and requirements you have for your partner. Better to do it before the marriage, and not after 20 years when your expectations are ruined. Because, by default, your partner will not follow your expectations, I can guarantee it.

You need to discuss the obligations that you have for each other. And if your partner will not follow these obligations, at least you have a moral basis for blaming him. But I can tell you that judging your partner is never a good thing. It is not an unconditional love for which all of us are looking.

But, if you think that your partner will act the same as you expect by default, this is not going to happen. This expectation comes from the fact that you treat him as if he is your own thing, like a purse. He is yours. This will ever lead to a healthy relationship in your life.

If both partners would be a self-lovers, there would be no requirements. The thing is that modern relationships are not about real love, they are about affection, attachment, addiction, maybe even gratitude, but not love, because actual love is always unconditional.

And this, in turn, causes several problems in life: fear to lose the object of your addiction, this fear leads to hatred, the hatred and fear causes jealousy, etc. In the end, those relationships will be most probably destroyed because we missed the main thing. You named it: self-love.

Nowadays relationships are a situation when two individuals who have no love inside their mind and soul are eager to get it from each other. In this situation the main problem is not even a lack of loving yourself, it's that people have no idea of what it is to love yourself. They think it's the same to become an egocentric.

If I accept myself, I do not need anything from anyone. I can only give love to the others, or decide that I will not give it. It's the same as money. If you have money, you can give it to someone; if you don't have it, you cannot give it to someone else. But there is a really no need for me to get love from the others. That's why relationships always start with loving yourself. If you don't have it, this is not a relationship; it is a form of affection, attachment and addiction.

Remember, self-love is a total acceptance of yourself, with all of your flaws. But if I change myself based on opinion of others, this is not self-love and not self-acceptance, it's a cause of different problems in life.

SECOND HALF

❖

The only thing that we learn in this life is to love

❖

If you treat yourself as a whole, you don't need a second half. Second half means I am defective because I am only a half. So, you then need to find a second half to become a whole and start to live happily. That's why all of us are seeking a second half. And when we find it, then we notice that our second half sometimes does not fit to the first half.

This whole idea is wrong. This myth is very dangerous and lies very deep inside the conscience of the people. People don't really realize this is wrong and everyone is busy seeking our second half.

Why this is wrong? Because the basis for this expression is the idea that I cannot be happy all by myself. This is impossible. Just think about it. This means that I am not good enough to be happy. There is something wrong with me being happy. I am just a half, not a whole. But, actually, you don't need a second half to make you whole Be the one to love yourself.

Having a thought that I am good enough to be happy and I need to find a second half to be loved creates an illusion of feeling as whole. When you find your second half you expect that everything will be perfect from then. That puts additional pressure on your partner and on your relationships and often becomes a basis of failing of these relationships.

Every human is a whole, not a half. And when you become a whole, then you will find a "second half."

But if you treat yourself as a half, not whole, you will find another partner who treats himself the same. And together, as a couple, you will not become a whole because this idea of being just a half means there is something defective with each you.

It is understandable that people want to find a love of their life to adore and admire as partners. The Internet is full of articles on how to find your second half and how to fall in love with your partner. And sometimes people ignore the fact that relationships are a process that have different stages of development. And falling in love is just a beginning of this long journey.

Of course, meeting your future partner is a great piece of luck. But would it be correct to say to we found our second half? Second half of what? One half of your desires and thoughts, and one half of his? Like there are no two fully similar apples in the world, there is no two exactly-the-same people. Even twins have differences. So, two are different, even though loving each other as individuals has not only similar but also different thoughts, dreams, hopes, and, most importantly, character. And if you fully merge yourself with another person's dreams and desires, even if you love him, you soon will find out that your self-love and self-respect disappears, proportionately increasing the importance of your partner. And suddenly that person finds out that he or she is physiologically dependent on the partner.

Any relationship creates some kind of emotional dependance because people inevitably react to the emotional feelings of their partner and get used to their partner's habits, tastes, and needs. And that's totally fine because when you love, you care about feelings of your partner. But, in a healthy relationship, there is always a space for your own needs, achieving your own goals and your personal development.

On the contrary, in emotionally dependent relationships, there is no such thing as personal space for free development of you as an individual. You depend on your partner by making him more significant than your needs, up to a full merger of your psychological spaces.

That's why personal life is source of unhappiness for many people. To prove my point, let's check the statistics: almost 50 percent of all marriages in the United States will end in divorce or separation. Over a 40-year period, 67 percent of first marriages terminate. The average first marriage that ends in divorce lasts about 8 years.

You can become a whole, not a half, only if you love yourself and accept yourself. If you have it, then your "second half" will be seeking you, not you seeking someone. Because people from all around the world seek happiness and energy and both of them is a result of feeling as a whole.

Only if you feel as a whole will you have love in your mind and soul, you fully accept yourself, and it means that others will accept you and love you. As you remember, your life is a reflection of your mind.

Only if you become a whole will you have the opportunity to become happy in a personal life. Otherwise, both of the partners will have an illusion of what personal life should be. And this illusion is not a reality and, therefore, disappears over the years. As you can see, loving yourself is fully connected to relationships.

Acceptance of myself means that I treat myself as a whole, not a half that needs another half to be happy. I am a complete person. There is a self-love in my soul and mind because if the person does not accept himself, there is no self-love inside him. If there is no self-love, no one will love him because people seek love and energy. That's why if there is no self-acceptance in the mind, this person is not complete. And that's why loving yourself is exigent for everyone, it's a basis of happiness in your life.

ACTION POINTS:

• What was your main motivation when seeking a new relationship? Were you trying to see yourself as a whole, not a half that needs another half?

• Try to find good things from the outside. In each person you interacted with during the day find 1 or 2 positive things. During the whole day pay attention to the positive aspects, ranging from a pleasant fresh breeze to the absence of traffic on your road to work. Learn to notice and appreciate what surrounds you. Write at least 15 positive points a day. Exercise also daily

RESULTS OF NOT LOVING YOURSELF

❖

Love must be sincere. Hate what is evil; cling to what is good.

Romans 12:9

A person who truly loves himself will never be drug addicted, an alcoholic, or a smoker. It's impossible for them. On the contrary, a person who doesn't love himself needs to have something in his life to feel "relaxed." People become drug addicted or alcoholics because of fear of reality. It's better for them to live inside an alcoholic illusion instead of reality.

Aggression is always a result of fear and fear is result of not loving yourself. That's why all the thugs, alcoholics, and drug addicts are just people who do not love themselves. And with that weird way they try to get love from the others.

And the real reason of all criminality in our society is that there is no God in a thug's mind and soul. Some of them might seem religious, but, in reality, there is no God inside them. They are not on God's list. Otherwise, they would love themselves and their life would be different.

Aggression is a request for love. Aggressive people are those who try to get love from others. And that's exactly why Jesus taught us how to respond to an act of aggression: "if anyone slaps you on the right cheek, turn to him the other also." Because the root cause of every act of aggression is a request of love, and love is always a best answer. As we know from this book, responding that way, to give love to the others, is only possible if you love yourself. This is where everything starts.

Fear is a result of not loving yourself. Our fears can be divided into two parts: fear of not getting love from others (fear of judgement or fear of loneliness) and fear of getting out of your comfort zone (fear of losing any material things, fear of trusting others).

Not wanting to face his fears, a person hides them under different masks, avoiding even to admit to himself of their origin. As a result, there is a painful experience, aggression, apathy, irritation, life in endless self-deception, dreams that did not come true.

It is worth discarding the veils that hide the roots of various fears; then a person begins to understand how much he has been influenced by negative attitudes that destroy his life ...

The first type of fear, "not getting love of others," is, in fact, self-hate.

Self-hate has many faces, it gives rise to fear of loneliness, fear of not being recognized, of insignificance, fear of condemnation, not realizing oneself, sometimes fear of living at all. As a result, a person burns out in emotional experiences such as anger, aggression, and hatred and spends his energy on constant self-assertion, playing for the audience, deep inside wanting to be loved as he is, without masks.

The second type of fear is the fear of leaving the "comfort zone," fear of losing "material things," fear of trusting the others; it is also a kind of self-hate for oneself, a misconception about oneself, distrust of oneself, the consequence of which is an unwillingness to take responsibility for everything that happens in your life on yourself.

If a person learned to love himself as he is, trusting himself absolutely, without a doubt, as the creator of his own life, he could accept any changes without fear, knowing that everything that happens is just a preparatory stage for the fulfillment of the desired. And then, what used to bring suffering would cease to frighten and cause such painful emotions

To change your life for the better, you just need to love yourself (accept yourself). To do this, you need to completely change your ideas about yourself. What are you? — A lot of attitudes, beliefs that lead to judgments, division into good — bad, good — evil, light — darkness?

Try to look at yourself not as a body, but as a creation of God, where not the body has you, but you have the body.

There is no good or bad, there is a whole, indivisible, one.

If I don't love myself and do to have a love in my soul and mind, I cannot give to the partner, I can only take. And that's why we seek a "second half" to take love from the partner.

The love that we seek in our second half is a projection of self-love. So, people in relationships are looking for love of themselves. But no one can love you more than yourself. That's why your partner cannot give you that which you are seeking. And that's why there are conflicts, miserable, etc. If a person truly loves himself, he does not depend on that. In this case, your relationships become an unconditional love.

There many real reasons for conflicts in the relationships. But the original reason is only lack of self-acceptance. This lack of self-acceptance causes finding your second half, which, as we discussed earlier, does not make any sense. But, after a while, these relationships will be over, for sure. This is a road to nowhere, because it starts without love of yourself.

So, if you really want to change your personal life, you need to look at original reason. Start with yourself. Concretely, accept 100 percent of yourself.

ACTION POINTS:

• While reading this book, you have probably already noticed the qualities and actions that are most difficult for you to accept in yourself or others. This also includes those things about which we say: "I will never act like that ..." or "I am not like that ...". When you hear or say these phrases, pay attention to the pressure with which they are pronounced, how much hidden energy is behind them. This is the energy of rejection.

• Make a list of everything that you do not accept in yourself and in others. Try to combine everything into a complete image. You can even sketch it.

CONCRETE ACTIONS

❖

Be kind and compassionate to one another, forgiving

each other, just as in Christ God forgave you

Ephesians 4:32

❖

It's very easy to love another person because our mind creates some sort of perfect image of this person, an illusion. But to love yourself is way harder because you know all of your flaws. That's why people tend to not love themself because we know we not like that perfect image. But when you meet your future partner, it's easy for your brain to create a perfect image and to fall in love with this image. But you cannot create a perfect image of yourself because you know you not perfect. And knowing the fact that you don't match with this image of perfection causes conflicts, stress, and depression. As I wrote earlier, depression is a self-hate that is a direct result of you not matching the perfection.

All the relationships, including all the problems in the relationships, were given to you by God to show you that you need to learn how to love yourself. That is the main purpose of life. You need to start by loving yourself.

What are the concrete actions of loving yourself? The first and foremost is self- forgiveness. You need to forgive yourself for not matching that image of a perfect you. Because just having that image of a perfect you is a sign of self-hate. If you fully love yourself, why do you need to be perfect? You accept who you are, you are totally happy with who you are. Otherwise, you are miserable because you have an image of a perfect you. And that's why you need self-forgiveness. You need to forgive yourself for being stupid. You need to forgive yourself for self-hate. Because of perfection, all that plastic surgery, correction of your body is all caused by self-hate. I hate myself and that's why I need to change myself. But you will never fully change yourself because plastic surgery will not change of who you are. If I accept myself, I forgive myself. And this is a first step. This will help you to feel not as a half, but full. To become full, you need to accept yourself, to accept yourself you need to forgive yourself. After forgiving yourself, you will realize that all the situations that required self-forgiveness ware very stupid. But until then, there will be no real happiness in your life because no other half will match with the half that inside your mind.

Forgiving yourself is not the same as forgiving other people, although both actions have similarities. When you forgive others, you have to open your heart to those who have hurt you. When you forgive yourself, you show, perhaps for the first time in years, love for yourself, even if you're not doing your best.

Take a fresh look at yourself. Yes, you are not perfect, but your guilt shows that you have good intentions now. If you have offended someone, you are ready to do everything to fix the situation. You are a unique person with your own worth. Try to endure the pain without destroying yourself or passing it on to others. Expect this process to take weeks or even months. You are performing soul rehabilitation, and any rehabilitation takes time. The process of forgiving yourself is much more difficult than the process of accepting yourself. You can end self-acceptance simply by accepting yourself as you are. When you forgive yourself, you rediscover your love for yourself and others.

Self-forgiveness is an approach to self and other people with openness, kindness, and compassion. This is the drive to give, not focus on yourself. Of course, self-love is not an excuse to continue the behavior that caused you to hate yourself. Don't play games. You are trying to change yourself, although you realize that your personality is more than certain actions at a particular moment. Repeat this healing mantra to help you forgive yourself:

I am more than the act I have done.

I accept myself and I can love myself as much as I love others. I know I am doing good to others.

I leave my self-loathing in the past as a big lie that has poisoned my life. I will never again be overcome by false feelings of guilt and self-loathing.

Since I am able to give love to others, I am able to give it to myself. The past no longer makes me suffer.

❖

ACTION POINTS:

• Write all the situations in your life when you felt guilty. Do you still criticize yourself?

• I encourage you to repeat the healing mantra from this chapter for those situations. Try to do it in the morning before the beginning of the work day.

• Think about how exactly forgiving yourself will help you to feel better, more energized, and happy in your life?

• It is convenient to start with the simplest. Take a piece of paper and write at least 10 sentences, each beginning with the words "I forgive myself for ...". List everything that upsets you in yourself, for which you are angry with yourself. Whatever mistakes you make, remember, you deserve to embrace yourself with them.

BE KIND TO YOURSELF

❖

A man who is kind benefits himself, but a cruel man hurts himself

Proverbs 11:17

❖

Another step of loving yourself is just be kind to yourself. Many of you notice that if something does not work or happen as you expected, you start to swear and become angry. If you think deeper, with whom do you think you angry? Of course, the answer will be that you angry with yourself. But why do you need to be angry with yourself if something goes not as you planned? Because you have an image of perfect you inside your mind that includes the image that you can do everything. And everything should go as you expected. All the psychologists and personal growth teachers insist that you can do everything, you are genius, etc. But if all of us are genius, it means that none of us are genius because average intelligence will be at the same level, although it will be very high. But this thought that you can do everything is a sign of not accepting yourself because none of us is perfect and when you face denial or inability to do something, it means that you are faulty. And that is exactly why you become angry at yourself.

And that's the perfect image of ourself that I can do everything lies deep inside our society. This leads to the situations where you become angry with yourself when something goes not as expected. And this anger is a sign of self-hate. Because there is an image of perfect you in your mind, where you can do everything, always, under any circumstances. This creates new obligations to be perfect.

If you think that you can do everything and you need to be successful in all areas of your life, you will be angry with yourself because of those obligations. And these obligations are based on your fantasies. What can be more stupid than to be angry with yourself? You can think about answering this question after reading this chapter.

In the end, every anger is an anger with yourself, because other people are inside your life, are a reflection of your mind. Everything that surrounds me is a reflection of me.

You think that everything has to be perfect but, in reality, God may put obstacles in your way and give you a power to overcome those obstacles. But, in reality, many of us do nothing for our life to be perfect. We expect it to be perfect, and when it's not, we become angry with ourself.

The more an individual expects his life to be perfect, the more he will be a shock when he faces reality. And that's a cause of huge stress in life, even depression, which in turn cause many physical illnesses.

If a person expects perfection from every situation in his life, when there is no perfection, he starts to analyze the situation and starts to blame himself. He thinks that if he would be smarter, taller, or have a more beautiful nose, everything would be perfect. But that is never the case.

So another step toward real self-love is to stop criticizing yourself. A person who truly loves himself and who truly accepts himself will never be angry when something goes not as planned in the various areas of life.

We are all human beings, we all tend to self-criticism, but why do some reach heights, while others do not? For you, criticism should be a kind of signal by which you will take a series of actions to correct this situation. And just criticizing yourself will lead to increasing the level of stress in your life.

Even if you fail, be your best friend. Think about the thoughts that dominate you when you've done things. Don't let these thoughts eat you up and destroy your sense of worth. Ask yourself: How would my friends / family support me in this situation? Then do the same. Even if you have stumbled, always be positive.

Take a break and relax. You probably know what will help you relax the best. Take a scent-oil bath, walk down your favorite park path, or have a heart-to-heart talk with someone. In general, whatever you wish. Your goal is to relieve stress.

Don't be upset or blame yourself over nothing. Even if it's something crucial don't be upset. We are all here to learn how to love. That's a purpose of life.

❖

ACTION POINTS:

• Look at yourself in the mirror and answer this question honestly: Do I really love myself? If it is still hard for you to give a clear answer to your question, don't worry. Keep practicing the actions from this book to help you get to know yourself better and on a deeper level, improve your relationships, accept yourself and others, solve different problems, and, finally, find God within you.

BIG MONEY

ENERGY

DIRECTLY

FROM GOD

MILLIONAIRE SECRETS TO ATTRACT YOUR PROSPERITY AND WEALTH

WHY I WROTE THIS BOOK

The paradox is that people do not know what money is -yet, money is a huge part of our lives. Nowadays, people cannot go anywhere without spending money or thinking about it; we often talk about money; we earn money. But what exactly is it?

Let's consider dollars. You go to the mall, take some green pieces of paper, and buy something. You give those pieces of paper and get some stuff in exchange. If, for example, you just handed over a random piece of paper from a book -nothing. Why is that?

The answer is that money is a material representation of energy. Because of that, money has energy. One dollar bill has one energy, and a hundred dollar bill has a different spectrum of energy. Each dollar bill is a piece of energy.

And that's why you can buy something in exchange for your money.

WHY YOU SHOULD READ THIS BOOK

You might believe it or not, but life is actually a reflection of your mindset. And money has a special room in your mind, too. If, in the part of your mind related to money, you will be poor or wealthy, it means that you will be poor or wealthy in real life. It's a reflection.

The thing is that it is possible to change your destiny. There is nothing determined in life. But to change it, you will need to have special knowledge.

For example, if you're not a specialist in computers, and your laptop is broken, can you fix it yourself? No. The same is true of life. To change your life, you will also need to gain special knowledge. Our lives are much more complicated than all of the computers combined. So, to change your life, you will need to have learned that additional, special knowledge.

If everyone understands that to fix your laptop you need to have expertise, but to change your life, which is much more complicated than computers, you will also need to have a great deal of expertise; many of us fail to realize it.

But when we start to change our lives, why are we surprised if everything is actually worse after the changes? We need to have some knowledge before we act; it's common sense. To change something in life, we need specialized knowledge.

This book contains that specialized knowledge as to money. And money is the second most important problem in our lives after relationships. We live in a world of money. And it is impossible for us to live without it.

MONEY IS ENERGY

Everything in our world consists of energy, because energy is everything that surrounds us. Everyone has heard about the energy of love, but does everyone know that the energy of money also exists?

Money is also energy, but it functions according to its own laws. Money is a material representation of energy. In fact, God invented and created money. Some deify money, some take it easily, some try to save it, and some live one day at a time and spend every penny made. Everyone treats money differently, but you must admit that money plays some role in each person's life, sometimes the main one, and sometimes secondary. And the amount that each person considers enough for happiness differs from person to person.

The energy of money has vibrations. We all know that any energy is not constant. Each of us feels vibrations of energy in ourselves. Money has a very powerful energy because so many thoughts from thousands of people are invested in it, because people crave money, curse it, love and hate it; therefore, money is saturated with great energy.

Unambiguously, money brings different types of feelings to people - joy and sorrow, freedom and captivity, pleasure and disappointment, power and powerlessness, stability and uncertainty, calmness and confusion. You need to clearly realize for yourself that money is not a goal, but it is just a tool to achieve your goals and fulfill your desires. You need to set your mindset to the thought that every year your income will increase, and if all you do is complain that there is no money or that you don't have enough, your energy of money will be tuned into your lack of money, since this is how you think. And vice versa, if you love and respect money and treat it carefully, do and do not waste it, then, the energy of money will be tuned in to your love of money, and, as a result, you will always have it.

Everyone should be able to determine the actual amount of money that he/she expects to receive within a certain period of time. Someone, after reading this book, will think that the more money the better. But this is not exactly true; there is a limit to what you can accept; the rest will be spent, wasted, lost, and you will not even remember how much and where it went.

The most important thing is not to think that in order for money to always be present in your life in sufficient quantities, you only need to want that to happen. Of course not, you need to do something more. You cannot become rich, just by waving a magic wand. You need to make an effort, and if money does not come right away, although you seem to work hard and a lot, you should not feel stressed and give up on your dream. And do not be greedy towards others; remember, if we do not give, then we will not receive. And you need to give (spend money) not with sad thoughts, but with joyful ones. You need to be able to share your wealth and not feel badly about it. When we give, we learn to manage the energy of money; when we spend it, and not waste it, we also manage this energy. Having mastered at least the most basic principles of money energy, your life will change.

YOUR LIFE IS A REFLECTION OF YOUR OWN MIND

We figured out previously that money is a material representation of energy. And here comes a very important question: What do you think comes first, money or energy?

The answer is energy. The life of a person is a reflection of his/her own mind. It means that the only things that might potentially happen to you are the ones that are inside your mind. And vice-versa, if you don't have something in your mind, it will not happen to you.

"Life is a mirror that reflects a person's thoughts. Why Should You Be Careful About Your Thoughts? Thought is the only way to order the world. However, thought can order the world so well that you stop seeing it." This is a quote from Ernest Holmes.

Later the philosopher added: "Thought is a screen, not a mirror; that's why you live in a mental envelope untouched by Reality "

This wise story, invented by Anthony de Mello, underlines this main message: "Life is a filter that reflects your innermost thoughts. People believe that external conditions are the source of their problems."

They are trying in vain to change the world around them in the hope that everything will improve. This rarely works because their thoughts continue to be in confusion"

American and French writer Anais Nin once said: "You don't see the world as it is. You see it as you are." The thoughts that are in your head come true regardless of your preference. Life is a mirror; it reflects what is happening within you. If you agree that the world is a mess, you will seek evidence to back it up. You can turn on the television and hear reports of accidents on the news, confirming your beliefs.

Another example is when people who were sick become healthy again; it can be the result of adopting a new mindset for healing. Albert Einstein once said: "We cannot solve our problems at the level of thinking that we were at when creating them." To improve conditions, you first need to reconsider your thoughts.

Life has a dualistic nature with many opposites. Days give way to nights, complementing each other. Without the dark of night, we would not appreciate the light of day. Some people adhere to the concept of free will. I believe that free will is an illusion. The term "free choice" rings truer for me. Life offers you feedback on the congruence of your thoughts, so you have the opportunity to correct them. "Think of the external environment as a mirror of your internal environment. When you observe something from the outside, for example, an event or a situation, look inside yourself to find reflection, parallel, connection. " said authors Charlene Belitz and Meg Lundstrom. Many people are dogmatic in their thinking and consider their thoughts to be fixed. This is wrong because millions of people have overcome their limiting beliefs to discover new possibilities.

Your life is a sequence of results, symbols, and shadows. There are no good or bad moments unless you have labeled them as such.

Reality provides feedback to help you to correct the mistake and create new circumstances based on changes in consciousness. Personal growth and self-improvement provide the path to lasting change if you are willing to do the inner work. You are the master of your own destiny. If you choose the victim role, life will surely provide you with evidence of this choice. Free choice means that life itself is neutral and ready to adjust to your thoughts. You are playing a game whose rules are not known to everyone.

Thoughts create the future "Everything that appears in our life is a reflection of what is happening within us." - Alan Cohen You create the future with every new thought. You have the ability to overcome any obstacle. The writer Neil Donald Walsh reminds us: "Life springs from your intentions. It is the fuel that drives the engine of creation in your life. " Negative thoughts shed light on your subconscious mind. They contain lessons designed to improve you and create a new reality. Life is a miracle based on universal laws. When you comply with them, you create circumstances in accordance with them. If you cling to negativity, you pull it into your reality. The cynic considers this improvement undesirable, and the optimist sees it as an opportunity to correct his/her own thoughts.

I like to talk about the connection between thoughts, emotions, and a person's life. Our thoughts turn into emotions, emotions give rise to events, and events lead to new thoughts - and so on, in a circle. And all this shapes our life.

Have you ever wondered what emotion is? There are many definitions, but the closest one for me is this: this is how your body feels a thought. What is an event? This is how space and time feel emotion. A thought? How the mind feels about an event.

All this is interconnected, one follows from the other, revolves in a closed circle, and is reflected in one another. It happens that a vicious circle is filled with negativity, and it seems that there is no way out of it. But it is within our power to open the circle and give the movement a different direction. First of all, we can change our thoughts - and they will affect both emotions and events. A great exercise for this is to ask yourself, "What will be the best result for me today?" Ask yourself this question every morning, and gradually, your thoughts will take a positive direction.

Remember, the world around you, like a mirror, reflects what you think and feel. And returns it to you a thousandfold. Whether you send fear and anger or joy and light into the world, you get the equivalent response.

What is reflected in your mirror?

ACTION POINTS

- Do you agree with the expression we discussed in this chapter? "Life is a reflection of your own mind." If you try to remember and analyze your previous experience, have you ever noticed how your mind influences the reality?

MONEY IS A CREATION OF GOD

Money always existed and will exist forever. Because money was created by God. During our life, we always interact with each other. Two things in this are always true: nothing is free, and nothing goes unnoticed. If you go to the grocery store to buy some milk, you must pay some money. If money didn't exist, this simple transaction of buying milk would be very hard to solve. In that case you, would interact with many others like farmers who produced this milk, sellers who sell the milk, etc. You would need to do chores and help them in order to get some milk from them. How could you get a milk in this situation? That's why God created money as a universal solution where you can get what you need and keep going.

You may solve your problems with money. Not every problem - but a vast majority of them. This is because money is a tool created by God to help you to solve problems through interactions with people. If you need to finish your business interaction with others, it is easier to pay them with some money.

And we don't even consider interaction with large factories, corporations, or banks; simple shopping would not be possible without money. That's why God created the way to help people cooperate with each other.

The ancients understood this very well: there will be no favor from God for you - your gardens will dry up, the fields with crops will be devoured by locusts, and robbers will steal cattle. And all your wealth will break into pieces overnight, and you will be a homeless, who will face a hole in debt for loans that you will have nothing to repay. To whom is God not pleased? Of course, to a sinner. Therefore, if you want to be healthy and rich, and not poor and sick, try to live in such a way to please God. The logic is quite obvious, and there are many convincing proofs of it in the Bible. In general, their meaning boils down to the following verse:

Moreover, when God gives someone wealth and possessions, and the ability to enjoy them, to accept their lot and be happy in their toil—this is a gift of God.

Ecclesiastes 5:19

Although, of course, it also happens that God sends trials to His faithful servants. A pious person can fall into disaster, his property can be taken away by villains, his good name disgraced. He can generally lose everything, including family and health, like the righteous Job. But in the end, the truth will still prevail, the righteous will again become rich and happy, and the estates seized by the villains will be taken away from them along with their lives, and the wealth they temporarily received will not bring them any joy in the end.

In the parables of Christ, it repeatedly sounds that all the property of each person is not his own property and is only temporarily given to him, but the true Master is in control of everything in the world.

Wealth is still viewed in the New Testament as a blessing of God, but it is constantly emphasized that the use of this blessing should be very responsible. If you decide that God gave you wealth only for your own pleasure, entertainment, and intoxication, then remember: The Master of this wealth will certainly ask you how you used the capital entrusted to you. This warning sounds most vividly in the t Parable of the Shrewd Manager (Luke 16: 1-9).

If you translate its contents into the language of modern realities, you get the following picture: a careless manager who squandered the owner's capital becomes aware of his upcoming dismissal. He writes off a huge part of the debt to the owner's debtors in order to secure their favor after he is fired. The owner learns about this fraud, but instead of punishing the fraudster, for some reason praises him for his thoughts.

However, all these misunderstandings are quite easily resolved if for a moment we digress from the plot of the parable and ask one single question: why does a master praise a servant? The answer is obvious: for fulfilling the will of the owner. But if the owner from the parable praised the steward for distributing his property to the debtors, it means that this is exactly what he expected from the servant. The manager was instructed to distribute the owner's estate among the have-nots, but instead he became greedy and began to spend it on his own needs. The owner considered this behavior wasteful.

Blessed Theophylact of Bulgaria interprets the Parable of the Shrewd Manager as follows: "The Lord here wishes to teach us how to dispose of the wealth entrusted to us well. And, firstly, we learn that we are not masters of the property, for we have nothing of our own, but that we are stewards of someone else's, entrusted to us by the Lord, so that we can dispose of the property well and in the way He commands. If we act in the management of wealth not according to the thought of the Master, but we squander what was entrusted to us on our whims, then we are such stewards on whom the denunciation is made. For the will of the Master is such that what we have been entrusted to us we use for the needs of our neighbors, and not for our own pleasures.

In other words, the manager was appointed to distribute, not to appropriate. Therefore, when he began to write off other people's debts at the expense of the master's estate, he did not deceive the owner at all, but simply returned to the performance of his direct duties. That is, he began to use what was entrusted to him for the needs of other people. And he earned praise from the owner.

Money has been created by God. That's why money is God. It means that everything that has been created in the world is God. That is why If you don't like money, you don't like God.

And this is again a very important concept. Because money is a tool created by God to help people to cooperate with each other.

HOW YOU TREAT MONEY

As we discussed, money is a tool was created by God. But how do people treat money?

If you treat money as something negative, if you think that money is the root of all evil or that huge amounts of money will poison your life, you will not become rich.

Life is a reflection of your mindset. And negative attitudes towards money stop you from running into a money flow from God. For example, can you become a good football player who earns tens of millions of dollars if you hate football? Fat chance.

If, in your conscious mind, money is a negative, then subconsciously you will do everything you can to avoid contact with this negative energy.

And this thought lies very deeply in our mind; so deeply, we may never realize or think about it. But my task here is to encourage you to think about it: if I don't like something, I will do everything to avoid it. Let's say if someone invites you to his place and beat you up really badly, you will not go there again. On the other hand, if you are welcomed somewhere with open arms, you would enthusiastically return. Subconsciously, you realize these truths.

So, the main problem here is that on one hand, everyone thinks about money, and we take many actions to earn it, and this is okay, but on the other hand, subconsciously, we have thoughts that money is negative.

And that's why there is a conflict; it's as if your left hand doesn't know what your right hand is doing, creating a problem with getting money into your life. Life is a reflection of a person's mind.

ACTION POINTS

• How do you treat money? Have you ever had thoughts that money is a negative thing in people's lives? Maybe you know examples from your own experience when big money led to lies, cheating, bribes, defamation, or even murder. Write your answers.

DO YOU LIKE MONEY?

Question: do you like money? Most probably, the answer will be "yes." Another question: how exactly do you demonstrate the love of money in your life? You might reply that you have your money safely in your beautiful wallet.

What emotions do you have when spending money? Do you spend with pleasure or regret?

The real love of money is when a person get pleasure from spending money and not when he receives money.

Of course, receiving money is also a great feeling. But the main question, is do you get pleasure when spending money?

I am sure each of you met a people who didn't really like to pay out. They can create a negative situation and continually try to postpone that payment. And if you ask them, "Do you like money?" The response will be, "Of course, are you kidding me?"

In the next chapter we will consider why these people who don't like to pay out demonstrate hate towards money and what exactly a true love of money is, but so far, I encourage you to spend your time thinking about the following action points.

ACTION POINTS

• Each time you spend your money next week, catch your thoughts and feelings when spending it. Is it a feeling of pleasure or regret? Be honest and write down your feelings

• If you have feelings of regret when spending money, it is okay. Continue being conscious of this, and the next chapters will help you to understand more about how to interact with the energy of money.

TRUE LOVE OF MONEY

The true love of money is not being attached to it. And you are not attached to money when you feel positive and joyful while spending it.

As I write in my book "Jesus About Loving Yourself: Religious View On Hot Topics In The Psychology," there is love, and there is affection, attachment, addiction, but not real love. This is more about relationships, but it's the same principle with regard to money.

To explain more about attachment, imagine that you walk in the woods and see a very beautiful flower. You cut it, bring it to your home, put it in the vase, and after several days, it fades. Another situation is if you spend several minutes admiring this beautiful flower, take a picture of it, and go away. The first situation is an example of attachment or greed and the second is true love or non-attachment.

True love is a state of mind where your mind and soul opens, and energy flows into your body. It's a source of energy for humans. And that's why everyone is seeking love in their lives. In reality, people seek energy, not love, because love is a state of mind when you receive more energy.

In this world, everything is made from love: people, subjects, events - the only difference is the frequency of this love. God created everything from love, because God is love. Money is also made out of love. Money is a material reflection of love.

So, if an individual does not feel great when spending money, then he/she is attached to it. And attachment leads to the fading of yourself just like the flower in the example above.

Attachment to money always leads to problems with money. It causes situations where the free flow of energy (money) stops. There will be no motion. And motion is energy, so when there is no motion, there is no energy.

If you feel difficulties when paying out, it means that you have an attachment to money. And just like any attachment, it causes obstacles to the motion of energy. In your own subconscious mind, you automatically set obstacles to it.

It is as if you were driving a car and pressed the brake and gas pedals simultaneously. And that is a relationship with money.

Here comes another question - are you happy when one of your friends buys a brand new, very expensive car? If yes, then ask yourself another question - do you really like and respect wealthy people? Honestly a vast majority of people don't really like them. Rich people for the government are already under duress: they pay more taxes, society expects them to participate in charity, etc. If a wealthy person goes broke, a lot of people feel happy about it, deep in their souls.

At the same time, no one wants to be poor. But if an individual does not really like rich people, even at a certain time, he/she will not become rich. This is how our mind works.

For instance, if I do not like golf, I will never become a good golf player. If a person doesn't like a wealthy people, but at the same time wants to be rich, this will cause stress in life. So, your relationship with money is not that simple.

If this person has two mutually exclusive attitudes in his/her mind, the result will be unsuccessful. But obviously, everyone in this world wants to be rich, and no-one wants to be poor. If you can recognize yourself in this person, don't be surprised if you don't always have the money you need.

All of this creates rejection of money deeply in a person's subconscious mind. If that person hates money, he/she will not get the amount desired.

ACTION POINTS

• Try to relax and very quickly, within a couple of minutes, without thinking for a second, without stopping, just on "autopilot," go write everything that comes to your mind about money and about your relationship with it.

• By the way, there can be quite a lot of information - for example, about two dozen sentences. The bigger, the better. Those thoughts can contradict each other, and among them, there may be those with which you cannot agree. But the whole point of the exercise is to splash out on paper what is actually, consciously or not, inside our minds.

• Then, look through your list of statements, noting (for example, with plus signs) those that are positive, as well as (minuses) statements with a negative meaning. Moreover, the negative can manifest itself in different ways. For example, it could be the fundamental "Money is the root of evil!" Psychologists say that such theses are very common as subconscious attitudes. It can also be a self-assessment of our relationship with money; for example, something like "Big money is not for me."

After that, you should calculate how many pros and cons are on your piece of paper. If you cannot boast of too much money, then the negative within you most likely, outperforms the positive, as reflected in your statements.

INTERACTING WITH MONEY ENERGY

Everyone loves to receive money - with this, perhaps, no one will argue. But often people have contradictory attitudes towards money. They love to hold the paycheck they just received, but they don't really like millionaires and other rich people. Why? Just because they have more money? This is the wrong approach. To create positive monetary energy around you, you need to love money in general, regardless of who earned it and in what quantity. If you have earned less than you have planned for a certain period, you cannot get upset and say that this amount is "not enough money for me." Be grateful for what you have now. If this is not enough for you, just plan your profits more carefully in the future.

Money is, first of all, a means of payment. You are paid for your work; you are paid for the satisfaction of your needs and desires. Money should be constantly circulating in your life. If you deserve a reward for something, accept it easily. With the same ease, spend your money when paying for your purchases. Money energy should be in motion, not stagnant. You can save money for a specific goal (preferably positive), and then this money will carry good energy.

Do not refuse gifts. Any material gift has some kind of money equivalent. If someone wants to give you something, do not refuse it, even if you think you are not worthy of such a gift. If a person presents you with a gift with a pure soul, without any selfish goals, then this gift will come to you charged with positive energy that the giver infused into it. Accept sincere gifts with gratitude; try to avoid insincere gifts whenever possible.

Some of us are embarrassed to pick up a bill or a coin from the sidewalk; some consider this an unworthy action. In fact, according to the law of monetary energy, it is possible and even necessary to pick up all the money found by chance. If you pass it by, you will thus show disrespect and disregard for money. And if you pick up even the lowest value coin and put it in your wallet, the flow of monetary energy will go straight in your direction.

Of course, money doesn't just appear in your wallet. You need to earn it. And the more carefully you do this, the more money will begin to love you. It doesn't matter how you earn it - by hard mental/physical labor or earning a percentage on your investments - you should always do it deliberately and purposefully. Take care of your income, and then, your income will take care of you

If you love money, you will carefully fold it in your wallet and always know how much you have. Respect for money is a very important quality, and the energy of money doesn't come to those who don't like it.

Also, the type of wallet affects the growth of money. If a person carries money in a pocket with holes or an old shabby wallet, he/she can forget about cash flow. A wallet made from natural materials in yellow, red, or brown works best.

Money loves order. Therefore, do not carry bills crumpled in your pocket, and do not shove them into small compartments in your bag. Always keep cash in your wallet. Fold bills at their face value - from highest to lowest, and do not wrinkle them. When you open your wallet, the bills should be facing you. Do not store different currencies (dollars, euros) in the same compartment, and also separate paper money from coins.

Your wallet is the so-called home for your money. And it, too, must be of the proper kind, clean and not torn. And never keep your wallet empty - there should always be at least one coin in there.

Otherwise, an individual may subconsciously try to get rid of money; it "burns" him or her. I've seen people who accidentally get a lot of money, and I feel that they wanted to get rid of it as soon as possible. They spend money on some ridiculous thing, which is the same as burning tens of thousands of dollars. Subconsciously, they try to get rid of money, and this is a sign of subconscious hatred of money.

ACTION POINTS

- Our task is to realize where we got harmful, negative attitudes; from whom, when, and under what circumstances, did we hear something similar. For example, maybe it was what your mother said, especially when she didn't want to buy something beautiful, tasteful, but expensive, or we heard negativity in answers to questions like: "Why don't we have a car?"

- Now that we know who the author of a particular belief was, it's time for the next step. It is necessary to analyze whether the author is an expert in the matter of handling money. That is, what does a family member who has never seen real wealth really know about money? Obviously, in this case, that relative was judging things that he/she did not understand, and therefore, those judgments, most likely are very far from the truth. Yet, we continue to carry those misconceptions.

ENDLESS AMOUNTS OF MONEY
IN THE WORLD

There is a common misconception that the overall amount of money in the world is limited. That is not true. Some of us think that we as part of the human race don't have enough money so not everyone is good enough to get money they want. That is an ideology of the political left (socialist) wing. If someone gets a lot of money, then some other person gets less money on the other side. And socialists thinks that everyone should earn equally.

In reality, the total amount of money in the world is endless because energy is endless. The source of this energy comes directly from God. And money is a material reflection of energy (love). Money is already in our mind in the shape of energy. And if you have the energy of money in your mind, it will attract the real money in your life.

But if you don't have the energy of money in your mind, it is impossible to attract money into your life.

This is a very important concept. Money is an effect, and energy in your mind is a cause. When people think about money, they always focus on where to get it. They think about dollars, pounds, euros, etc. In their minds, money is a piece of paper or numbers on their credit cards. But it is all effect, not cause. It leads to a classical scenario when people don't have a clear understanding of what is cause and what is effect and are unable to see the truth.

You get paid for your work, and money is a reflection of energy. That's why people do not get money they want, because they focus and expend all of their energy not on cause but on effect.

If you want to get more money, you need to focus more of your energy on the cause of money, not on the money itself. You will not achieve money for free because everything in this world is made out of energy. Physicists know that the law of conservation of energy states that energy can neither be created nor destroyed - only converted from one form of energy to another. So, even if we consider free cheese in a mousetrap, the cheese there is not free because someone bought this cheese and put it into a mousetrap. And even if the cheese was not purchased, someone made the cheese out of milk, so that person spent his/her own energy, which is equivalent to spending money.

We should focus on energy that leads to money. If you focus on money, you put obstacles on energy movement since you are focusing on the wrong things. If we want to get rich, we should not think about money; instead, we should focus on the process that leads us to money.

THREE MAIN ASPECTS OF MONEY

The energy of money can be viewed as three main aspects. Just like a person, money can manifest itself on the physical, emotional, and mental levels.

The physical manifestation of money is the most understandable - it is bills, coins, as well as credit cards. They need to be treated with care and respect. Money needs a house, which is a wallet. You shouldn't keep your money in your pockets, just in your bag, or put it on the table. Put money straight into your wallet, dividing it into large, small and coins by department. Turn all bills with the front side with the number plate facing up, so that when you open the wallet, you will see exactly what you have.

On an emotional level, your attitude towards money is expressed. What do you feel when you get a large amount in your hands; what exactly do you need it for? Try to always be aware of the amount that you own. Money loves order. Therefore, regularly recalculate your savings, in this way you will get rid of stagnant cash flow and attract money energy.

The mental level of money energy manifests itself in your thoughts. Watch your thoughts and words about money.

If you constantly think and say that there is no money, that you are always short of money, that you cannot afford expensive purchases, then it will be so. After all, you program yourself for poverty and shortage, according to all the rules of psychological self-hypnosis:

- Thinking constantly.
- Say it out loud.
- Speak in the present tense.
- Believe it firmly.
- Reinforce with true emotions.
- You instill this in yourself every day for a long time.
- And your subconscious mind has no choice but to agree with your undeniable belief.

What to do in this situation? You need to change your thinking and attitudes. Eliminate all thoughts associated with a lack of money and replace negative thoughts with the opposite.

Do not think negatively about money, and do not condemn those who have it, because it is a negative attitude, resentment towards life circumstances, and envy which lead to even greater losses and despair.

Any energy, including the energy of money, is initially neutral, and people themselves endow it with positive or negative qualities. Someone sees temptation in money, others as a means of paying off debts, a third thinks that, as it comes, it will also leave, etc.

But remember, at the beginning we learned that the main principle of money energy is exchange? So, you need to perceive it this way. Everything that you know how to do, all your talents and abilities can be associated with money energy. And when you stop thinking about money only as pieces of paper, you can join the cash flow and use this energy to build your well-being and prosperity. The more energy, the more opportunities for the realization of what you desire.

ACTION POINTS

- It is also very important to understand whether you are ready to accept money in your life right now. How much and how will you spend it? What are the risks involved?

- If you just want a lot of money, do not know what to spend it on, are afraid of loss or theft, do not want anyone to know about it, etc., then you are not yet ready to launch the energy of money into your life. And why do you personally need money? Think and write down the reasons on paper.

WEALTH AND POVERTY: DO YOU HAVE ENOUGH?

What is wealth, and what is poverty? The fact is that people measure everything by money now. Wealth and poverty are an amount of money in someone's mind. For example, if you make a certain amount of money, you're poor. If you're lucky to make more money, then you're rich. There is always a threshold in people's mind, and everyone has his/her own threshold.

But is it actually true? No. Probably in every company, there are people who have different salaries. And sometimes, there are people who make less money actually have more money in their bank accounts than those who earn high salaries. Those people definitely spend more money, sometimes on alcohol, gambling or drugs. Casinos, alcohol, and drugs are a 'vacuum cleaner' of money.

The truth is that wealth and poverty do not equal the amount of money in one's bank account. Wealth and poverty are a state of your mind. If I think in my mind that the amount of money I have is enough for my lifestyle, then I am a wealthy person. It doesn't matter how much I have. On the contrary, if I think that I don't have enough money, despite being a millionaire, then I am a poor.

So, in reality, wealth and poverty are a state of mind. And this state of mind leads to the thought of whether you have enough money or not. If you have enough, you're rich. Otherwise, you're poor.

To give you an example, if a 'poor' person bought a bicycle and a 'wealthy' person bought a yacht, and they spend all of their money on this purchase, neither has any money left in their bank accounts. The 'rich' person is happy with purchasing the yacht; he easily spent his money without being attached to it, and the 'poor' individual, although happy with having a bicycle, feels really sad because he doesn't know how he can buy food for dinner.

The amount of money itself does not really matter. What really matters is whether you have enough money or not. If you think you have enough money, you can relax; you're a rich person.

The thing is that desires of the individual are endless. It's not possible to satisfy them all. There is not enough money to satisfy all our desires. Therefore, if we choose to satisfy all of our wishes, we can't get enough money, and we are always poor!

We *will never have enough amount of money to satisfy all our desires. Our desires are endless.*

And this is a very important concept because it solves a very important problem in our mind: someone is wealthy, someone is poor, poor people are greedy and want wealth from rich people, rich don't like poor etc.

In reality, both rich and poor measure their wealth in money, not by the feelings of whether they have enough money or not. So, how to get rich depends on -whether you earn more or spend less, it may be better to spend less since this means you have lowered your desires.

ACTION POINTS

• The actions described are beyond the scope of one book. Therefore, it is incorrect to call them an exercise - this is more precisely - practice. Instead of the most "harmful" negative statements that you wrote earlier, it is necessary to compose positive ones. For example, the accusatory "money is the root of evil!" can be changed to: "Money is a power that allows you to do a lot of useful and good things." These positive statements cannot be formal; they must find a live response within you, so you may perceive them emotionally.

• And then we follow the directive: "Practice makes perfect." Positive statements must be constantly repeated, every day, focusing your attention on them many times. But this is not enough - they need to be consolidated into practical actions, matching what they say. For example, you suggest to yourself that "money is a tool for good deeds," so do something good even with the little means that you have. If you are working with the statement, "I deserve big money," then, every day take some steps that can lead to that money, at least in theory.

• A positive statement will gain a foothold not only as a thought, but also as a practical skill, for which you need at least 40 days of repetition.

CONSUMPTION

People often purchase things not because they need them, but because other people bought those things.

Today, in the era of consumerism, people buy many things they don't really need. If you don't use something in your house for a year, it is better to get rid of it. But I am sure all of us have such things. Some of us store unnecessary things in our garage or in other rooms.

The modern economy and advertising in general work to artificially increase demand. Promotion of products follows a simple scheme: an attractive image creates an illusion that if we buy this product, we will be able to get closer to the image in the picture or achieve the life we always dreamed of. In the context of fashion, everything works the same way. We see photos of bloggers on social networks or in an advertising campaign with beautiful models, and we think that buying a bag, shoes, or a dress will make us as successful, beautiful, and desirable as the heroines or heroes who promote them. However, in reality, everything is much more prosaic: many fashion must-haves look great on models and not very good on ordinary people like you and me.

First, try to adequately evaluate, the suitability of what's advertised for the ordinary person, and then decide if the fashion trends or other items correspond to your lifestyle. Living in the modern world, it is impossible to completely remove yourself from the pressure of advertising, but you can control its impact.

Since the mass market was at the forefront of the fashion industry, the process of producing and consuming clothing has taken on enormous proportions. The statistics are frightening: more than 80 billion wardrobe items are consumed annually in the world, and in the United States alone, the volume of textile waste is more than 15 million tons per year. Cheap clothing contributes to the fact that now we can buy more with low prices increasing demand at times. It is tempting to be able to possess a lot of things for relatively little money, but this is often just deceiving in nature. Just figure out how much you paid in aggregate for a dozen t-shirts that became unusable after a couple of washings, synthetic dresses that turned out to be impossible to wear in the heat, and synthetic leather shoes that don't suit your feet.

We need to understand that more does not mean better. You do not need to completely abandon the mass market, but approach shopping wisely: read the components of clothes and examine the quality of the seams, the relevance of the item for the next few seasons and it's convenience. It is often much more economical to buy one thing which is more expensive, but of better quality, than several cheaper things. This rule also applies to sales: you shouldn't spend money on something just because you are offered a 70% discount or greater.

Often, we go shopping with no purpose - to unwind, spend time, or cheer up. Such situations most often lead to impulse shopping: you buy something but have no idea why. But buying just for the sake of buying is almost always impractical: most likely, what you bought will just hang in your closet forever. Psychologists believe that the process of buying something makes us feel more important - I can buy it, therefore, I exist.

Try not to go shopping (online or offline - it doesn't matter) when you feel bored or are in a bad mood: the feeling of wasted time can force you to buy "at least something," so as not to leave the store empty-handed. Do you remember that experts advise not to go grocery shopping on an empty stomach and need to have a list of essential foods with you? It's the same here; before shopping, make a list of the wardrobe items you need/want to buy and follow the plan. The more detailed the description of the item (dress with a floral print of midi length, black straight-cut trousers with a belt), the lower the chance of a miss. But do not deprive yourself of the opportunity to go beyond the established framework; what if instead of jeans for every day, you come across the perfect jacket that you have been looking for forever, and it's even priced right? As a last resort, you usually have at least two weeks to return it to the store, so remember to keep your receipts.

CONSIDER MONEY AS A TOOL, NOT A GOAL

Money should be considered as an instrument. It should be considered as a tool, not a goal.

But the vast majority of people do not understand this concept. For them, money is a measurement for pretty much everything. But money is a tool of life. The amount of money you have should be enough to achieve your goals, matching what you plan to do.

Therefore, this very important concept follows:

The amount of money people have is always enough.

For example, when someone really has a need to reach his/her goal, and if this person does not have enough money to achieve it, money shows up from nowhere: maybe an old debt is repaid, a bonus appears, or some other event results in that money. This happens because the money that is needed appeared in that person's mind.

It is not easy to calculate your costs and plan your budget when even the thought of money produces fear and anxiety. If the numbers at the end of the month never match, you may simply stop trying to keep track of your expenses and income. But once you think of money as a tool, you can focus on solving a problem rather than being emotional.

It all starts with an important goal for you. Money itself is not a goal. You need to know what you want to spend it on. To feed your family? Pay off debts or cover medical expenses? Travel? When you know your goal, you can plan and spend to achieve it. For instance:

- Sell something to save up for a rainy day.
- Write a plan for ridding yourself of all debt in two years' time.
- Make a list of where to look for another job, because now you are not as scared to leave your unloved place of work. (We will talk about this later.)

The main thing is to learn how to use your means in such a way as to live the life you want. Here are some practical tips.

Since money is not a goal, you need to know what exactly your goals are. This is why many financial planners start out with a client with a single question, asking "why?" When you know the answer, all of your financial decisions are made in line with your goals.

It is also very helpful to make a list of the expenses that give you the most pleasure. This will also help control costs. For example, if you like to dine in a cafe and visit family or friends living in another city, you could make that a priority and decide where you need to cut other expenses.

When your income is very low, changing your attitude toward money is especially difficult. In comparison to your income, goals will seem unattainable. So, break your goal down into smaller steps. For example, if you need to repay a loan, don't think about the entire amount, but about the number of payments each month or even per week. So, the amount will not seem completely unmanageable. It will be easier for you to pay it back and feel like you are in control.

For many of us, money means more than it really should. and reminds us of what we are missing. What we can't afford. But, in essence, money is just a tool. Try and treat it as such. Of course, this will not change your financial situation in just one day, but this way, you will begin to control your finances.

ACTION POINTS

- Have you ever had a goal to make 'X' amount of money per year? If yes, I encourage you to start considering money as a tool instead by doing exercises described in this chapter.

THE NATURE OF A LOAN

Let's consider a typical situation: a person wants to start a new business and tells his friend that he has a brilliant idea. Just $1000 and soon, we will have a million. So, he asks his friend, or maybe a bank for a loan.

In reality, you don't need start- up capital to start a business. To start a business, you need energy and nothing more! This energy will attract the money you need. Almost every business that is based on borrowed money for its start-up capital will not end well.

You may object and say that large companies sometimes get loans, but that is a totally, different situation since their loans are for working capital. It means that today they produce the product, ship it, and in two days they will receive payment, but they need the money tomorrow. That's why they get loans from banks. Plus, usually their huge teams of financial analysts consider and calculate the risks on a very high-level.

From this perspective, getting too large a loan is not an option. Would you lift a weight that is too heavy for you while working out? Could you even lift it? No. It's because you are trying to lift a weight that is above your current physical capabilities. The same is true with an oversized loan; you receive money above your energy capabilities. In reality, you are not receiving money. You are receiving energy!

So, I encourage you to be very careful with your financial liabilities. I know that a huge number of people in 2008 were not able to pay their debts just because of this mistake. So, to avoid being caught in the same trap, it is better to pay off your debts in advance if you have some extra money in your bank account, even ten dollars' worth, to pay off loans. It's a good idea, and in addition to the psychological benefits of reducing your debt, you will enjoy measurable financial satisfaction.

Try to pay your debts down as soon as possible. It is a simple strategy, but almost no one really follows it. Usually, people save up some amount of money and then send it to pay off debt.

So, from an energy point of view, a loan is something that you need to get rid of as soon as possible because it means that you have exceeded your energy capabilities. This causes stress. It means that you don't have enough energy, and this stress might lead to problems in your life, including your health.

Money is energy, and your job is to clean up your cash flows from all sides. If funds are not enough and if you live on a below average salary, it means that there is little energy as well. First of all, you need to enhance your financial thinking.

Now, here's the point. Energy is taken away by debts - both your own and those owed to you by others. I understand that it is difficult to live in modern world without loans, but somehow, I live without them and quite successfully. When someone owes you, that person uses your energy. And when you owe someone, you use someone else's energy.

No one knows what is going to happen tomorrow. But do you think that those people who get a bank loan for 20 or 30 years know what will happen during in such long period of time? Do you think they can all predict future like magicians?

So, I suggest you take out any loan very wisely, especially if it's high interest or for a long period of time. If you're not 100% sure that you will pay off your debt, don't take it. You need to learn how not to live beyond your means.

If you take out a mortgage, it doesn't really mean you own that house, since the house is an asset of the bank. You are just allowed to live in this house, but this is not your house and if you do not pay your debt, and bank takes "your" house back. It will truly become yours only when you pay off your mortgage. And this is a very important fact that many people do not understand.

Banking loan in general is a product from bank that you buy. Bank is selling you money. Basically, when you take the loan you buy money (energy) from the bank. But you pay more energy to the bank because of interest rate.

We have no other choice but to get loans or use banks. That's why many people have problems with paying their debts because they don't know how much energy they have in their mind. But even having a huge amount of money in your bank does not guarantee that you can use those money. Sometimes even large banks go bankrupt. For example, in 2008 25 US banks failed. in 2009 this amount increased up to 140 and in 2010 there were 157 failed banks in America.

SAVE ENERGY, NOT MONEY

Why do people try to save money? The answer is fear. Fear that tomorrow will be worse than today. But every action based on fear will always end badly. It means that if you save money for the future, it is based on fear that tomorrow's situation will be worse than today's, so, as a result, the situation will be worse in real life.

If a person tries to save money for retirement in his/her 20s, it means one is acting like God, because only God knows what will happen in 40 or 50 years. If in 2006 someone would have told you that in two years, we would face the largest financial crisis since the Great Depression, would you believe it?? Of course not.

The U.S. financial crisis led to a global financial crisis followed by the European debt crisis, which began with a deficit in Greece in late 2009, and the 2008-2011 Icelandic financial crisis, which involved the failure of all three of the major banks in Iceland, and, relative to the size of its economy, was the largest economic collapse suffered by any country in economic history.

If such a giant ship as the global economy sank, what can we say about the life of one individual? It is just a tear in the ocean of the global economy.

I suggest not saving money, but instead saving energy.

Energy is a cause, and money is an effect, a reflection of this energy.

If you save money, you save pieces of paper or just numbers in your bank account which may become almost nothing over a long period of time.

You may want to ask, what does it mean to save energy? Let me explain. What do you think you get paid for? For actions that lead to results. Actions are a demonstration of energy. So, the algorithm is the following: you have energy in your mind, and you have a goal, that you spend your energy towards, and you have a result (money) that you achieve by spending your energy. Therefore, we have three elements that are based on energy: actions, results, and money that you get for these results.

Energy is cause, and money is the effect. As I mentioned, the main issue here is that people mismatch cause and effect. If you spend your energy on actions, your actions will always result in earning money.

Saving money in your 20's for retirement is not a sound financial policy because many people do not live long enough to retire.

CAREER ADVICE FROM GOD: CHOOSE THE RIGHT CAREER PATH

Do you like your job? If yes, did you really choose it by yourself or it was it a circumstance in your life?

A vast majority of people chose their occupation when they were teenagers or in their early 20s. The main issue is that most probably that choice of occupation was not made by us. It's made by our parents, or recommended by our friends, or someone else has influenced our choice. Most probably, our choice was made based on the wages paid. For example, doctors and accountants usually earn more than electricians and drivers.

The very common situation is when a child graduates high school, he/she is not really interested in studying a specific field. So, it doesn't matter which occupation he/she will choose, and the choice is often made by the parents. Kids don't know which career path will be best for them, so parents take the responsibility to decide or at least give advice. But what do parents actually know about their kids? Not so much. So, the decision is usually made by wages paid, leading to career paths such as lawyers, doctors, or economists.

So, the common practice is that parents or society influence your decision to become a doctor, and you work as a doctor, but you don't really like your job. And, as a result, people do the things they dislike on an everyday basis, leading to a miserable life and stressful situations.

But how can you figure out if you like your job? And the answer is very easy. When you go on vacation - are you happy? If you are happy, then sorry, you don't really like your job.

Being a "holiday person" or trying to start a new life on Monday is a vicious path. Sunday usually finds us relaxed and Monday graciously invites us to get back on track. Whichever day of the week is today, one thing is clear: if something does not suit us in life, we are allowed to change. Change something now to wake up with a smile tomorrow.

Where to begin? Start with your own feelings. In one of the discussions about the secrets of happiness, philosopher Daniel Dennett once said: "Find something more important than you and devote your whole life to it." The recipe, as you can see, is simple. Another thing is that the discovery of this "important" goal is a task no less difficult than the search for the meaning of life.

Probably the biggest problem in self-determination is false values: often we want wealth, but do not know what we will do with it; sometimes we strive for fame, not thinking what we can give to the world. As a result, odd jobs come into our lives which bring money but cannot make us happy, popularity makes us famous but lonely. In confirmation of this – there are thousands of wealthy people who have forgotten how to enjoy life. This phenomenon is discussed in detail in the book, "Sex, Money, Happiness and Death: In Search of Yourself, " written by renowned psychologist and management specialist, Manfred Kets de Vries, about the wealth fatigue syndrome.

An all-consuming passion for things and material goods leads to the fact that a person seeks to "possess," not "live."

It mixes wants and needs, and this is what the entire advertising industry is built on.

Steve Jobs' speech, which he delivered in 2005 to Stanford University alumni, has become a classic. But you should periodically refer to other classics as well in order to discover new and new meanings for yourself:

Your work is going to fill a large part of your life, and the only way to be truly satisfied is to do what you believe is great work. And the only way to do great work is to love what you do. If you haven't found it yet, keep looking. Don't settle. As with all matters of the heart, you'll know when you find it. And, like any great relationship, it just gets better and better as the years roll on. So, keep looking until you find it. Don't settle.

Lewis Hyde became famous as the author of the great book about creativity "The Gift: Creativity and the Artist in the Modern World,", which was published back in 1979. Despite the age of the book, the advice given has not become outdated.

Here are Hyde's reflections on the difference between work and creative work:

"Work is what we do by the hour and, if possible, for money. Welding parts on an assembly line, washing dishes, calculating taxes, making rounds in a mental hospital, growing asparagus is work. Labor, on the contrary, sets its own rhythm. We can get a reward for it, but it will be harder to measure it ... Creating a poem, raising a child, developing a new method of calculus, overcoming neurosis, inventing something is work."

If you really like what you do for a living, you will not get tired of your job. The more you love your job, the harder you'll work. "Do what you'll love, and you'll never work another day in your life." It's a well-known sentiment.

ACTION POINTS

- Do you really love your job? Answer honestly
- Try to remember how exactly did you make your career choice? Under what circumstances - what did your parents and friends tell you? Have you been undecided?
- Did you choose your career path based on the wages paid or based on what you really love?
- Do you still think you made the right choice?

WORK AND IT'S INFLUENCE ON YOUR HEALTH

Another question is, how often do you get sick? The person who likes his/her job rarely gets sick. So, work is a rest, and rest is work for such people. Work is a possibility for the free movement of energy. That is why if an individual loves what he/she does for a living, he/she will achieve results and earn great amounts of money no matter what.

Those who don't like their job get sick very often. They will do everything to not go to their jobs. Because by working on such jobs, they destroy themselves. They destroy their health. If a person does what he/she doesn't like, serious health issues will arise. Working on a job that you don't like causes stress and disappointments in your life. And that is a basis for getting sick.

Studies conducted in various parts of the world show that only 25-30% of the population love their jobs, 12%

even hate their jobs, and the remainder don't like their jobs.

These numbers make you wonder how many people are suffering every day. Moreover, suffering is not limited to bad moods and unwillingness to go to an unloved job but can result in real health problems.

Australian scientists have proven that the impact of work on human health is enormous. And not loving your work can bring irreparable harm to our body.

You may have already encountered the following health problems, which are associated with chronic stress:

- problems with the cardiovascular system, for example: pain in the heart, arrhythmias, increased blood pressure, vegetative-vascular dystonia;
- disruptions in the nervous system: headaches, insomnia, irritability, depression;
- digestive disorders: impaired appetite, nausea, abdominal pain, for example, gastritis, cholecystitis, colitis;

- problems with the musculoskeletal system can be disturbed by pain in the back and joints. There are cases of paresis (weakness) of the limbs;
- respiratory problems: from frequent "colds," diseases, such as pharyngitis to bronchitis, and even asthma attacks.

The seriousness can vary from functional disorders (minor temporary disturbances) to actual organ damage. However, it is very difficult for doctors to establish the cause of the pathology, and it is almost impossible to find an effective treatment. Prescribed painkillers and sedatives (sedatives), as well as antiarrhythmic, hypotensive (lowering pressure), anti-inflammatory drugs do not give any results.

This happens because all these diseases are classified as psychosomatic, that is, they are caused by psychological causes, so traditional treatment can only lead to temporary improvement. The severity of the illness may depend on the duration of the psychological impact, i.e., how long you force yourself to go to a job you hate, performing tasks that make you feel sick, literally and figuratively.

You may not like work for various reasons. The negative impact of work on human health is not diminished just because there is a good reason to go to an unloved job. For example, it doesn't matter if you entered college at the insistence of your parents, for the company, or you just need to feed your family; the effect on your body is manifested in the same way. If you are not indifferent to your own health, and work prevents you from living happily, then think about what is more important to you.

A person who loves his job will spend much more energy at his job, and we know that we have an algorithm of energy- actions- result. So, the more energy you have, and you will have more energy if you like your job, the more results you will get.

GOD'S TASK: FALL IN LOVE WITH YOUR JOB

So, the question is how can I love my job that I didn't choose? That's a tricky question. Maybe I like a job that doesn't pay good wages. Now I will say that you need to love your job any way. If you already love what you do for a living, you can close this book. You will be rich anyway. Otherwise, your task is to fall in love with your job no matter what you do for a living.

It is not a coincidence that you work at your current job. It means that you should accept it. You may believe in destiny or not, but every situation that humans face is created by God, and therefore is perfect for that individual. It is just a reflection of your mind.

It is really your task to fall in love with your job. Because if you can fall in love with a job you don't really like, you can do every job in your life. It means that you will get better results in your career and even more broadly, in your life.

But how can we fall in love with our jobs? And the answer is that we need to focus on doing our best. This is a task. You can be a top manager or truck driver; the task is to focus on doing your best for a business.

Whatever you do for a living, every individual must do the best at his/her job. This is a task from God. If you not trying to do the best at work, it means that you not doing what God wants you to do with your life, and most probably you will lose your job, and the next job will be worse than your current one.

Each of us must focus on doing our best, and this is a task from God. Focusing on doing your best has the power to transform your life. Whether in athletics, business, school or any other activity, focusing on doing your best always makes you feel like a winner.

Doing your best is a task from God if you believe in Jesus, or Allah, or Buddha; it does not really matter, I suggest you focus on your God when working on your job. For example, if you are washing dishes, imagine that you are doing it, not for yourself, but for your own God, to make God happy. If you are an accountant, you do your job not for yourself or for the company you work for, you do it for God, and you see God in the process of work. And if you truly believe, and therefore love God, you will do your best at any job.

So, in the evening at the end of working hours, we must ask ourselves one question: "Did I do my best today or not?"

If a person loves something, energy flows freely. Because love is a state of mind where your mind and soul open up and energy flows into your body, it means that you have more energy in your life. Love is a way to get energy. Therefore, if an individual does not love his/her job, there is no free flow of energy. It means that this energy flow stops inside of him/her and destroys that person.

Whatever you do I encourage you to do your best at work, it is a task from God, and it is a way to improve your life.

ACTION POINTS

• Keep a special career journal. Every day, at the end of working hours, make a detailed book entry answering the question "Did I do my best today or not?" What exactly were my tasks for today?" Could I make improvements in my work or interactions with my coworkers? If yes, make a plan for such improvements.

• Imagine if a group of scientists were tracking you all day long, counting and evaluating every second of your life. Then, they pass all the information they collect to you and tell you what you need to change to improve your life. How valuable their advice would be! This is what your journal will do.

TO BE PRESENT: LIVING IN THE HERE AND NOW

All of us either live in hope for the future or by thinking and remembering the good old or bad days from the past. So, we are nowhere; we don't live our lives, because for that, we would have to be present in the here and now.

If a person does his/her best at work, it means that he/she lives in the here and now and does not think about what might happen in the future or what took place in the past. You might do your best at work only by being present, opposed to doing average work if you are thinking about the future or about the past.

That is why doing your best at work is a way to transform your mindset, improve your life, and get better with regards to your health, because it requires you to live in the here and now.

Isn't it a wonderful skill to enjoy every moment, every second? Yes, having your thoughts in the past or in the future is a habit that many people are infected with. While being on vacation, instead of relaxing and resting properly, their thoughts are at work, or on worries about children left at home with their grandmother. After returning home, they begin to remember their vacation, looking at the photos and regretting that the time had flown by so quickly. Another situation is when a person is at home, but his thoughts are solving workplace problems. And while at work, a person indulges in thoughts about household chores.

When a person is absorbed in yesterday or tomorrow, the present is elusive. Happiness is either here and now or not at all. If we are not here and not now, then where are we then? There is no past, and never will be - it has already passed. The future will never come, because when we get closer to it, it changes its status to the present. And the present is every minute living in the here and now. It is life, and life is only in the present.

To live in the here and now, know where you are striving and what you want in the future. Easy to say! After all, life is an endless river of different kinds of occasions and events; it's an unstoppable stream which requires you to personally decide something, go somewhere, or do something. Of course, in this life it is necessary to plan and foresee something and calculate in advance. But it's important to keep balance in everything.

Learn to deal with problems as they arise and not to deal with them when they disappear. Don't worry about things that haven't happened yet, and don't worry about things that don't concern you. If you are driven into a bad situation, without any positive result, tell yourself, like Scarlett from the movie "Gone with the Wind": "I'll think about it tomorrow." And, in some cases, you shouldn't even think about it tomorrow. Ideally, you are the one who chooses what you think.

The general perception of life is made up of small, accidental feelings, images, experiences that are happening to us today. To live is to experience every moment - to be who we are now. Accepting our true self here and now, we are able to experience the beautiful, to feel the joy of every moment of life, i.e., to see how the snow falls, so weightless, soundless or when a titmouse flies in, sits on the porch rail, and looks at us.

We suddenly notice the shaking of a branch in the open window, or a light of the morning sun, or a drop of rain on the windshield. And this small thing shifts our mood - from being bored, anxious, empty inside to a little pleasure. All the REAL things around you can be interesting or evoke thought or sadness. And you are a part of such a big and such a small world. Indeed, the ability to manage your thoughts, appreciate the present moment, and be happy is the art of life.

ACTION POINTS

- **Body Scan Exercise**

This simple exercise is a great way to get yourself into being present and get in touch with your body. Doing this in the morning can also help you get your day off to a good start.

While sitting up straight or lying down on your bed (just make sure not to fall asleep if you try this lying down!), take a few deep, mindful breaths. Notice the way your breath enters and exits your lungs.

Starting with your toes, focus your attention on one part of your body at a time. Pay attention to how that area is feeling and notice any sensations that you are experiencing (Scott, n.d.). After a few moments of focused attention, move up to the next part of your body (i.e., after your toes, focus on your feet, then ankles, then calves, etc.).

This is not only a good method for putting you in a being present state right off the bat, it can also help you notice when your body is feeling differently than normal.

You might catch an injury or illness that you wouldn't normally notice, just by taking a few minutes each morning to scan your body.

NEVER ARGUE WITH YOUR BOSS

Never argue with your boss, because even if you 'win', you lose

Very often each of us discuss the decision made by management and by your boss, and sometimes we disagree with them or even argue with them We think that we would do a better job or make better decisions. And that is not exactly correct because if God put you into this situation, and you have a boss, this boss was given you by God.

It doesn't really matter if your boss has a different approach in doing business or if he/she is, in your opinion, doing stupid things. At the end of the day, you can become a boss by applying to a manager position or open your own business as an entrepreneur. It's a very easy approach to life.

Another issue related to careers is that everyone is not very happy with how much money they make. We think that our salary is lower than we want.

We always get paid what we deserve.

If you think that you get paid is not what you deserve, nowadays, it's very easy to find a new job with maybe more responsibilities, but a higher salary. If you can find a better job, you truly deserve more. But in the end, only the market will decide if you do; we alone cannot make this decision. Otherwise, falling in love with your current job and doing your best will help you to improve your career.

If you are not happy with what you get paid, you are not happy with the results. As we discussed earlier, we have an algorithm: energy- actions- result and focusing on energy will bring actions into your career and help you to achieve better results and make more money in the end.

Don't get me wrong; you have a choice to disagree with how much money you make, and if you are able to find new job, you are correct. But otherwise, you deserve what you get paid. In any case, the market evaluates you correctly. I am sure not everyone will like this idea, but only the market can tell if your desire to get paid more is realistic.

Another common complaint about the job is that employees think that they work really hard and that they have a much more demanding task on their desk than others. But the thing is, if you do many tasks at your work, and your area of responsibility is huge, your boss must trust you.

The more tasks on your desk, the more you are trusted. It is a very good thing, because in case of financial problems or financial crises, your job will survive because of this trust. Even if you get fired, you will find a new job very soon, and it may be better than your previous work.

If you are looking for a way to earn more money, it is best not to ask for an increase to your salary but instead ask for more responsibilities. You will do what your other coworkers don't do, and you will be viewed by your boss as a proactive employee. Any manager would love that!

In my experience, the most valuable employees are the ones who are proactive. They control situations by causing things to happen instead of sitting and waiting to respond after things happen. Proactive individuals don't sit around waiting for answers to appear; they stand up, put one foot in front of the other, and find the answers. They don't wait for someone to hand them an instruction manual; they are resourceful.

ACTION POINTS

• Think about how falling in love with your job influences your perception of your boss, your coworkers, clients, and anyone else you interact with.

• If you would be a boss, and you would have an employee who truly loves the job, doing his/her best at the office and never argues with you, always gives constructive feedback, while being proactive, and asks for more responsibilities, would you consider promoting this employee? That's why seeing salary increase as an effect, not a cause is a common misconception in our lives.

3 THINGS FOR YOUR BUSINESS TO BE SUCCESSFUL

The same thing holds true regarding a business. The main issue is that everyone wants to become a millionaire immediately. But in business, the most important thing is not money. Remember, money is an effect, not a cause. There are three things that are most important in any business: energy, a very clean understanding of what you going to do (business plan), and willpower to get things done.

But being an entrepreneur doesn't mean making a lot of money. I know people who make 6 figures by being employed, not including bonuses such as shares of the company they work for - sometimes annual bonuses may exceed yearly salary - and I know entrepreneurs who make about or even below a median wage, while working much more than regular employee. So, it is not that easy.

I know that nowadays many of us want to become an entrepreneur and be our own boss, and it's a common misconception that you need nothing but startup capital. Running a successful business is not only about money; it's about ideas and energy and willpower to get things done! If you don't have these attributes, money is not going to help you in any business. You will spend it and be lucky to escape without loans. If you have those three things, your business will be successful.

HAVE A GOOD BUSINESS PLAN

An independent, internal business development plan is drawn up to achieve maximum efficiency from the implementation of the conceived idea and is an action plan to achieve certain indicators. In the business plan, it is imperative to include information about the resources already available and what else needs to be obtained (financial resources, team, access to production resources, etc.).

In the internal business plan, you need to write as many alternatives as possible, and try to focus on the best ones.

The internal business plan also helps you, as manager of the company, to make management decisions.

Recommendation: Try to hire an outside expert to draw up an internal business plan, maybe a more experienced entrepreneur from a related industry, to give you a fresh perspective on business prospects.

Remember, external people will be considering your plan. For example, a potential investor may need to make a decision to provide financing for your business project. Therefore, it is necessary to clearly convey the consistency of the product, its demand in the market, as well as the benefits that the investor will receive. The more detailed the business plan, the more attractive your project will look.

A good external business plan should answer these questions:

- What is the company's product?
- What are the prospects for the market in which the company operates?
- Analysis of competitors and potential risks
- Product development vision
- Financial model and development plan

Depending on the investor, you will need to be less or more formal about your business plan.

For example, if you are a startup looking for an investment from a venture capital fund, then a simple business plan can be in the form of a presentation that you prepare yourself, containing the key points of the business plan. The form of the presentation will not be important to that investor; the main thing will be whether it is sufficient for making a decision. Make sure it is understandable and well-structured.

At the same time, if you are the owner of large company that wants to get a loan from an institutional investor, then you need to write a 20-30 page document that will be 100% consistent with the template of that institutional investor, up to matching the fonts and size of the text of the business plan.

Before you start creating a business plan for your project, you need to do the preparatory work: systemize all the information you have and study financial data. If at the preparation stage you see that there is not adequate information, you can reach out to specialists to evaluate the company or work out the missing aspects yourself.

A business plan for creating an enterprise/ company/ startup may look like a presentation or a text document, but, in any case, it is important that it contains the following information:

- Brief summary of the project
- Description of the goals of attracting investments
- Market Description
- Company description and company product(s)
- Marketing plan
- Organizational plan
- Financial plan
- Risk analysis
- How to bring the work started to the end result

We need to understand the reasons we may be diverted from our intended goals.

Why don't we finish what we started and keep our promises? There are several reasons:

1. We don't have enough energy to complete what we wanted to do, and we sour on the project due to fatigue.

2. We do live responsibly and fail to finish what we start, even to protect our reputation.

3. We become bored doing the same actions, and we give up our undertakings for the sake of something else - something that seems new, interesting, and attractive.

In the next chapter, we will discuss how to bring the work we start to a successful conclusion.

HOW TO GAIN WILLPOWER TO ALWAYS GET YOUR WORK DONE

This is an art and skill in itself: the more often a person manages to finish what he/she has begun, the smoother life will become.

How to bring that work you started to its proper end? There are several fundamental principles to follow:

- Try to link your state of well-being and happiness to the quantity and quality of the completed work. Imagine a person who says - I did everything I could and at the same time basically finished everything that I started Such a person will be a happy person, regardless of whether old or young.

- Try to make the business you are devoting your time to, inspire you. If it is rather routine, try to include it in larger life projects that seriously inspire you.

It is easier for spiritual seekers and religiously- minded people to be inspired, because their whole life is an exciting and endless process of improvements with more of a mission.

• Find your inner self responsible for achieving the results and bringing the project to an end. Let it become your corporate identity, your habit, and part of your image.

• Master the skills needed to perceive each business as a type of process with an internal rhythm, in which there are zones of activity, along with less active zones.

These zones in different systems are called either biorhythms, or successful astrological days, or ascending and descending octaves, or flow states.

When everything is good, and we are in a positive flow, then we can reduce our own activity and just try to keep this state.

When it is difficult and we are fighting for the result ourselves, then we need to make conscious efforts, waiting out the difficulties or striving to find this favorable flow.

Life is a circumstance through which we pass. Try to complete each cycle of the work begun, each ring, without leaving incomplete ones behind.

Each case consists of certain bricks - micro-elements, micro-cases, micro-circumstances, and they must be done with respect and thoughtfulness.

Make a list of unfinished tasks and make the absolute decision to live without liabilities: it will be much easier for you if you do this. It is possible that the dead ends of your life, formed due to incomprehensible reasons, are actually generated by unfinished business. Make a list of these to-dos and gradually close them down, one-by-one.

If you want to learn how to bring the things you have begun to an end, you need to make both external and internal efforts.

With external efforts, everything is clear, you have to repeat a set of actions over and over again to get the needed result.

For instance, if a person needs money for urgent expenses, then he/she will consistently do those actions, either by working harder and trying to make money, by getting a bank loan, or by borrowing money from friends or acquaintances.

What can be a distraction from such actions? Changes in mood or doubts about meeting goals are just two possible internal deviations from your path.

But even when a person gives up due to being carried away by other external affairs, the root of this issue must be sought within him/her.

Therefore, for successful completion of the work, it is not enough to make a decision one time, and then act.; you need to repeatedly remind yourself of the target and about the actions to meet that goal.

We need to create a clear image of the future result, which motivates us to implement our plans. It is also necessary to find balance between purpose and pleasure, to love the process of overcoming difficulties as the most important work of life, thus strengthening our willpower muscle.

You need to form your willpower inside you; your willpower will be responsible for the achievement of the concept by periodically evoking the image of yourself as a successful, effective achiever.

You can't get distracted from the goal and forget about it, being carried away by something outside. The only permissible distraction is a temporary rest, in order to recuperate and rush forward to achieve the cherished milestones.

To complete the work you have begun, go through all the micro-stages of your actions, perform with quality, and do not give up the reins of your life.

Then, you will become the real Lord of the Rings of your own destiny and complete the cycle of your earthly existence with a sense of accomplishment and happiness.

Create a clear mental image of the ending, or the result that you wish to obtain. Enlarge this image in size and view it as if under a magnifying glass. Try to mentally climb this mountain peak and experience the enjoyment of the victory won.

Tune in to the fact that the movement along the micro-steps towards the goal should be pleasant: for this, spread the feeling of joy that you have when you mentally reach the finale throughout the entire process of conquering the goal.

Of course, we are talking about some serious abandoned life projects and not that you put off buying a burned out light bulb and prefer to sit in the dark. Think about from the height of your still virtual victory, which path will be most relevant?

You must choose the best, shortest, most effective solution. Walk mentally along the stairway built in your mind several times until the program becomes clear to you and until there is a feeling of completion, as if you have completed a circle.

Imagine that as you approach an abandoned target again, you draw a circle or connect a broken line. It is important that this line is filled with inner content for you, and that this practice does not turn into only visualization exercises.

Feel that you are internally connected with the goal and your path to it is returning home, receiving an inheritance by right, getting what you want naturally, as if the prince, upon reaching a certain age, becomes a king.

Create an image of yourself with the qualities of strength, able to overcome any obstacles and conquer any peaks. When sketched out in your mind several ways to complete what you started, pick the one that is closest to you.

And, most importantly, take action. Try to get up from the computer right now and start the process of completing some unfinished business.

Also, try to make a decision and after a week, cut the backlog in half. If weeks are short, then plan to do it in two or three weeks, but do not stretch it out to a month or more.

So, let's start to complete what we started and what we did not finish. Observe yourself and carefully study all thoughts and feelings of resistance.

There is nothing more beautiful than feeling free from debt.

ABOUT THE AUTHOR

Writer, blogger, and activist Mike McArthur is an expert in philosophy of religion, quitting addiction, unconscious mind, psychology of loving yourself. He derives satisfaction from helping people find happiness and in encouraging them to lead healthy and meaningful life

OTHER BOOKS BY MIKE MCARTHUR

How to Easily Quit Smoking by Hacking Your Subconscious Mind: A Life-Changing Guide to Smoking Cessation and Healing Your Life

ONE LAST THING

If you enjoyed this book or otherwise found it useful, I'd be very grateful if you'd post a short review on Amazon. Your support really does make a difference and I read all the reviews personally so I can get your feedback and make this book even better.

Thanks again for your support!

Printed in Great Britain
by Amazon

67619554R00108